Live Television
Time, Space and the Broadcast Event

Stephanie Marriott

SAGE Publications
Los Angeles • London • New Delhi • Singapore

First published 2007

SAGE Publications Ltd
1 Oliver's Yard
55 City Road
London EC1Y 1SP

SAGE Publications Inc.
2455 Teller Road
Thousand Oaks, California 91320

SAGE Publications India Pvt Ltd
B 1/I 1 Mohan Cooperative Industrial Area
Mathura Road
New Delhi 110 044

SAGE Publications Asia-Pacific Pte Ltd
33 Pekin Street #02-01
Far East Square
Singapore 048763

Library of Congress Control Number: 2007925095

British Library Cataloguing in Publication data

A catalogue record for this book is available from the British
Library

ISBN 978-0-7619-5909-0
ISBN 978-0-7619-5910-6 (pbk)

Typeset by CEPHA Imaging Pvt. Ltd., Bangalore, India
Printed in Great Britain by TJ International Ltd,
Padstow, Cornwall
Printed on paper from sustainable resources

For Steve, for bearing with me

Contents

Acknowledgements

This book could not have been written without the encouragement of fellow members of the Ross Priory Group for Research on Broadcast Talk. Thanks in particular go to Martin Montgomery for inviting me in the first place, and to both Martin and Joanna Thornborrow for organizing the annual seminars. Members of the group over the last decade – Joanna, Martin, Andrew Tolson, Kay Richardson, Greg Myers, Arnt Maasø, Espen Ytreberg, Helen Wood, Nik Coupland, Trudy Haarman, Richard Fitzgerald, Peter Lunt, Shoshana Blum-Kulka, Paddy Scannell and others – have consistently provided intellectual stimulation and direction, and excellent company as well.

The book has been a long time in the making, and a number of colleagues and friends helped to sustain it along the way. Particular debts of gratitude are owed to Myra Macdonald, for reading the final draft and stopping me from giving up along the way, and to other good colleagues both at the University of Stirling and elsewhere, most especially Jane Sillars, Tim Thornicroft, Suzy Angus, Philip Schlesinger and Karen Lury, all of whom provided invaluable support at key moments.

Thanks are due to the Department of Film & Media Studies at Stirling for the study leave which allowed me to complete the research. I gratefully acknowledge the support of the AHRC, whose Research Leave Scheme provided the time and space to finishing writing the book.

Last but not least, special thanks are due to Steve Marriott, love of my life, for his patience and good humour in the face of my endless footering about.

Part I
Time and Space

1

Mediated Interactions

1.1 Introduction

On 31 December 1999 the BBC, in conjunction with 50 other broadcasters, launched what it described as a 'complex and ambitious project on a scale never before attempted in the history of television':[1] a 25-hour live broadcast during which more than 2,000 cameras around the world, operating across some 60 satellite paths, would follow the build-up to midnight country-by-country as the international dateline moved west across the globe and the year 2000 dawned in each location in turn. The aim of this project, repeatedly declared by the BBC over the course of its live coverage, was to deliver to its viewers nothing less than 'the world' in its entirety:

> In one revolution, in one day, we bring you the world. Wherever you are, whatever you're doing, the BBC is with you on *2000 Today*.

The *2000 Today* broadcast was by no means without its problems. Presenters tossed to correspondents around the world who were not on camera, could not be heard or were out of sync; live feeds failed to materialize, or were lost in mid-segment. The broadcast, furthermore, seemed destined to disenchant, given its goal of delivering the moment of midnight over and over again around the world. If midnight on New Year's Eve is a liminal moment, a transitional moment made meaningful for individuals through the particularities of their own time and place, their own cultural and personal context, then the serial manifestations of midnight in Kiribas, in Auckland, in New York, in Paris and elsewhere could only serve to depreciate the value of the viewer's own midnight; a risk which the presenters seemed to recognize in their repeated and persistent references over the course of the day to their 'own millennium midnight', the upcoming 'real' moment in the UK.[2] Viewed from this perspective, the subsequent comment in one British newspaper lambasting the 'wreckage of the BBC's millennium coverage' seems easy enough to comprehend.[3]

To view the *2000 Today* programme simply in terms of its limitations, though, may be to miss the point. As one of the anchors remarked, some twelve hours

---

[1] BBC Press Office and WGBH National Promotion, 6 October 1998.

[2] On liminality, see Turner (1969: 95), who likens liminality 'to death, to being in the womb, to invisibility, to darkness, to bisexuality, to the wilderness, and to an eclipse of the sun or moon'; see also Marriott (2001).

[3] *The Guardian*, 4 September 2000.

into the coverage, there was at least one perspective from which the programme
could be regarded as extraordinary:

> When I first started television ... I'm sure this would've been absolutely totally
> inconceivable; there's no way this could have happened at all. I mean, about 50 miles
> was as far as you could go, wasn't it, and now in a very short period of time you've got
> this absolute miracle ... it's extraordinary to think you can actually encircle the globe
> like this electronically.[4]

The presenter Michael Parkinson's comments here make clear the nature of the
rhetoric which underpinned the *2000 Today* broadcast: a celebration of what
Carey (1989: 139) has referred to as the 'electronic sublime', the dizzying
imaginings of the transformations in human communication which can be
delivered by technologies of communication. Whilst *2000 Today*, in other words,
may have run the risk of dispossessing the domestic television audience of their
'own millennium midnight' through the incessant reiteration of other midnights
in other places, it had a different variety of enchantment to offer instead: the
enchantment of 'the world', everywhere simultaneous and everywhere articulated
through electronic communication. The liminal moment which television sought
to capture in its transmission of this event was thus not simply the moment of
midnight as it would manifest itself in the UK some hours into the live broadcast,
but also the transition between one millennium of technological progress and the
next, marked by the 25-hour flow of images and talk from a multiplicity of
simultaneous elsewheres. Self-reflexively, repeatedly, television was celebrating
the transformations it had wrought in human communicative potential.

In this book I will be examining the repercussions of these transformations,
with a particular view to the shifts that the development of electronic forms
of communication has brought about for our experience of time, space and
interactivity. Several writers (e.g. Hjarvard, 1994; Stevenson, 1995) have noted
that such transformations in our experience of time and space have received little
in the way of detailed attention. It is this 'chronically under-researched area'
(Stevenson, 1995: 114) which this book will investigate, via a consideration
of the defining features of electronic communication, and of live television in
particular.

The choice of live television as the subject of this book may appear to require
a degree of justification, given the consequences of media convergence. At the
time of writing, individual television programmes can be consumed via digital
download, and live television can similarly be streamed to a computer or a
mobile phone. Why, at such a point in time, would a book on television be
a worthwhile expenditure of energy, for either the reader or the writer? The
answer, in part, is that the book concerns itself with television as a medium, and
not with the apparatus itself; the arguments therefore hold equally true whether
we are considering the consumption of a live broadcast in a living room via a
traditional television, on a computer screen in an office or on the street via any
one of a number of personal media.

---

[4]Michael Parkinson, BBC1, 31 December 1999.

Why television, though? And why live television in particular? The analysis in this book will reveal that live television is quite extraordinarily complex when viewed from the perspective of the transformations that it brings about in our experience of time and space. Previous writings on broadcast communication have tended to focus on two significant aspects of the way in which both television and radio deliver their messages. One of these is the institutional context in which television and radio are produced (Scannell, 1991, 1996), which has as its consequence the organizational involvement in the communicative event of parties other than the immediate participants; the other is the production of broadcast talk for an overhearing audience (Heritage, 1985: 99; Heritage and Greatbatch, 1991: 96), and more specifically for what Scannell (1996: 174) refers to as 'anyone-as-someone', an audience which is typically unknown but which is nevertheless addressed in its particularity. As this notion of the overhearing audience makes clear, broadcast communication is produced primarily for a hearer who is absent from the place in which the talk is produced, and who may be distant in time as well; but the space-time complexities which arise from this distanciation of the audience from the site of the communicative event have rarely been discussed in detail. When compared to radio, television is particularly interesting from this point of view because of the visual context for the communication, shared by television performer and remote audience. This is neither trivial nor insignificant in its range of possible effects; where radio messages are dependent on and constituted by aural communication alone, television involves a range of additional extralinguistic contextual factors: the physical make-up of the place in which the talk is produced, the physical behaviour of the speaker, visual access to other places with their own aesthetic and spatial characteristics. With live television, furthermore, co-temporality – the sharing of the same present moment – exists as a perpetual ontological possibility, realized whenever the broadcast is 'live' in the full sense that the time of the event, the time of television creation and the time of transmission and reception are one and the same (Heath and Skirrow, 1977: 53). Taken together, these characteristics – the institutional character of the broadcast event; its production for a non-specific but momentarily particularized absent audience; the presence of a perceptual space which may be more or less shared between speaker and absent audience but which minimally involves some visual domain which is known by the performer to be available to the viewer; the potential for the instantaneous transmission of information across distance – define the context in which televisual communication is produced and received. Jointly and severally they give rise to a range of interesting phenomena, which it will be the task of this book to investigate.

The investigation in this book will centre around the work of mediation which live broadcasting carries out in its transformation of the stuff of the world into the material of the broadcast event. It is the mediation of the event which bestows upon it the spatial and temporal complexity which will be discussed in what follows. In realizing the event, live television restructures the world both in space (the relations between the place in which stuff happens, the place from which the event is spoken and the places in which it is received) and in time (the temporal architecture of the event, in which the everywhere-simultaneous world is structured into convoluted and dynamic reconfigurations of past and present in the real time of the live broadcast).

Such restructurings, as I will argue in Chapter 2, do not bring about a change in the nature of the universe. Space does not shrink, when electronic communication permits absent participants to engage in immediate interactions with each other; nor does time run backwards, re-loop or reconfigure itself. Rather, the transformations of time, space and patterns of interactivity which will be examined in this book are shifts in our *experience* of the world, permitting us to encounter events from temporal and spatial perspectives other than those available to us in a face-to-face interaction.

It is this transformation of our encounter with the world which will be crucial to the arguments developed here, and as a consequence the book will adopt a phenomenological approach, with a focus on the way in which live television, through its real-time mediation and realization of the situation, performs the event as a particular kind of object of experience for its audience. Central to this endeavour will be the approach advocated by the phenomenological sociologist Alfred Schutz, insofar as the book will seek to 'bracket' (Heritage, 1984: 41; Schutz, 1962: 105) or temporarily put to one side taken-for-granted views of space, time and interactivity in order to construct a bottom-up analysis of the phenomena under investigation. The purpose and value of such 'laborious analyses' (Schutz, 1962: 100) should become clear as the book proceeds with its construction of a grounded underpinning for the argument which it will be developing.

I will begin this task in the remainder of this chapter with a consideration of the differences between face-to-face and electronically mediated interactions, which will permit us to develop an account of the spatial characteristics of instantaneous communication across distance. This will be taken forward in Chapter 2 with a similar consideration of time.

1.2   The Face-to-Face Encounter

Mediated encounters – encounters in which some or all of the relevant participants are absent from the immediate situation, dealing with each other instead via an intervening medium – differ in significant ways from face-to-face interactions. In the face-to-face or 'canonical' situation (Lyons, 1977: 638), participants are in the same place, and can potentially see, hear, touch, smell and even taste the same objects. Avery and McCain (1986: 122) define seven sensory modalities, all of which can potentially come into play in a canonical encounter: audio verbal (hearing or listening to speech), audio non-verbal (hearing non-speech sounds), visual verbal (reading), visual pictorial (looking at images), olfactory (smelling), tactile (touching) and taste. The possibility of jointly accessing all of these modalities will depend, of course, on the size of the place in which individuals are co-present: at a large-scale event such as an open-air concert or festival, a person several hundred metres away from me will not be able to read what I can read (unless we are both reading it from a video screen) or smell what

I can smell (unless the aroma of fast-food is omnipresent in our surroundings). If we consider a more finite and bounded space such as a room, however, it becomes clear that objects in the immediate vicinity will offer themselves to the entire range of sensory modalities for all those who are co-present. A poster on the wall can potentially be seen and read by anyone in the room; speech, unless it is whispered, will be available to anyone who is able to listen; my companion's recent lawn-mowing will be available as both a visual and an olfactory stimulus (the flotsam and jetsam from the garden sticking to his or her shoes; the smell of freshly cut grass). Furthermore, as 'embodied subjects' (Merleau-Ponty, 1962: 318) – individuals who are necessarily in the world and of the world – the more of our senses that we can bring to bear upon an object, the more fully we can realize it. Take as an example the kind of optical point-of-view shots that occasionally turn up in films made for IMAX screens. The huge IMAX theatre at Niagara Falls in Canada, for instance, features a film on the history of the Falls in which a camera mounted on the prow of a boat permits spectators the illusion that waters are surging over their heads. This may induce a degree of claustrophobia or dizziness in the audience at the apparent immediacy of the experience; nevertheless, one need only step out of the cinema doors to encounter the Falls themselves and experience the difference between being 'at grips with the world' (Merleau-Ponty, 1962: 303) in all its sensorily experienced fullness on the one hand and the thinness of seeing and hearing a torrent rush towards one on a screen on the other. To be present in the immediate vicinity of an object, then, is to have the fullest possible sensory access to it.

Full co-existence with objects and individuals, furthermore, as Husserl argues, involves not only the kind of totalizing unity of the senses that Merleau-Ponty talks about but also the engagement of the 'kinesthetically functioning living body' (Husserl, 1970 [1936]: 106), with its experience of its own 'body position, movement, weight, muscular tension and suchlike' (Hammond et al., 1991: 159): an ineffable and irreducible sense of ourselves and of our own immediate embodied situatedness in space and time. The individual who comes blinking out of the movie theatre and into the sunlight at Niagara will not only hear and see the spectacle, taste and feel and smell the spray, but will be possessed as well by an ineluctable sense of their own *hereness* in the particular environment in which they find themselves and in which other objects and circumstances – the waterfall, the crowd, the sunshine – are co-present. In this context we can usefully draw on Evans' (1982: 167) argument that individuals cannot conceive of two separate places simultaneously as 'here'. Developing an elaborate conceit around the idea of a remotely controlled submarine on the seabed which is equipped with limbs and excavators, Evans asserts that even though the observer might, in such cases, be able to reference a remote object as 'this' or the place where it was picked up as 'here', this is by no means the same as actually conceiving of oneself as being there:

> The subject can *play* at being where the submarine is ('Here it's mucky'); he can *play* at having that mechanical contrivance for his body ('I'll pick up that rock'). But really *he* is (say) in the bowels of a ship on the surface of the water. This is not just one

view he can adopt if he likes; it is the view to which everything in his thinking points. (Evans, 1982: 166, original emphases)

Individuals, Evans continues, must conceive of themselves as actually being *somewhere*: we cannot at the same time perceive the world from two points of view (1982: 168). However caught up we may momentarily be in the stimuli offered by a situation remote from us, then – even in the case of immersive virtual environments – we nevertheless always persistently find ourselves to be in the location where we are watching, or listening, or speaking: our maximal commitment, both sensory and kinaesthetic, is to the place *where we are*.

This primary orientation to conditions of presence reveals itself most clearly in *deixis*, the linguistic system that permits us to indexically identify places, objects and individuals relative to our own situatedness in the world.[5] The most basic use of expressions such as 'here', 'there', 'this place', 'that place', for instance, is to index places in relation to a zero-point centred upon the speaker's own corporeal engagement with the world: 'here' means 'in this place', where I am at the moment in which I utter the word 'here'; there means 'that place', where I am not.

Deixis, furthermore, in its most fundamental uses, appears to require not only presence but also *co-presence*. As Lyons remarks:

There is much in the structure of languages that can only be explained on the assumption that they have developed for communication in face-to-face interaction. This is clearly so as far as deixis is concerned. Many utterances which would be readily interpretable in a canonical situation-of-utterance are subject to various kinds of ambiguity or indeterminacy if they are produced in a non-canonical situation ... if the participants cannot see each other, or cannot see what the other can see.

(Lyons, 1977: 638)

The use of deictic expressions, in other words, presupposes that the indexed element is intersubjectively available to all relevant participants; and there are a range of uses where only co-presence, apparently, will do for establishing the relevant common ground. An earthbound individual cannot felicitously refer to an object ten miles away as 'on my right', because the object will be out of visual range and so inaccessible to those co-present; but a plane pilot, producing a commentary for passengers, can advise them to look out of their windows and view an entire town ten miles away 'on the left'. Conversely, we can point to the moon, when it is visible, and expect any co-present individuals to understand us when we claim that 'no-one ever really landed *there*', but we cannot point up the motorway from London and refer to Glasgow as 'there'.[6] 'What does *this smell* remind you of?', addressed to a friend on the phone, is likewise assured of an infelicitous outcome, as is the question 'does my bum look big in *this*?' directed at an individual in the next room.[7]

---

[5] See Bühler, 1982; Fillmore, 1975, 1982; Levinson, 1983; Lyons, 1977; Rommetveit, 1968, 1973.

[6] Looser constraints attend the 'symbolic' use of deictic expressions; cf. Fillmore's example of a telephone conversation in which the speaker asks whether Johnny is 'there' (Fillmore, 1975).

[7] Although the latter may well have a particular speech act function, that of requesting that the hearer come into the room *where I am* to see which outfit I'm referring to.

So-called *gestural* uses of deictic expressions (Fillmore, 1975: 40), further-more, require more than simple co-presence. 'Does my bum look big in *this*?' may well be doubly infelicitous, requiring not only a co-present audience but one who is actively monitoring the speaker's indexical behaviour as she gestures in the general direction of an item of clothing or a part of her anatomy. The only thing which would stand between blindfolded listeners and a disaster in such a situation would be whatever reserves of tactfulness – or irritation – they could muster. When deictics are used gesturally, being co-present isn't sufficient; relevant participants need to see what is being indicated if they are to make sense of what is said.

Co-presence is thus a fundamental condition for the optimal interpretation of a range of deictic uses of language. It is the shared vicinity, in all of these instances, which supplies the relevant common ground for identifying the indicated object, individual or event; and a *co-operative* speaker (Grice, 1975) will reserve their use of deictic expressions for those circumstances where other relevant participants will share the appropriate common ground, whether this be the locale-at-large or a particular demonstratively identified object.

The cardinal property of the canonical situation – the potential for all co-present individuals to jointly access the full range of sensory modalities on offer – thus has as one consequence the use of a range of linguistic expressions that permit participants to identify and locate elements in their vicinity – sounds, smells, sights, tastes – relative to the sensory and kinaesthetic zero-point which is *where they are*. Other behavioural and interactional features are similarly consequent; but whilst the gestural use of deictics involves the *physical* indication of some local element, other sets of cues, both non-verbal and verbal, operate at a more symbolic and expressive level. Participants who can see each other and – more to the point – who know themselves to be seen, can indicate via facial expressions what their attitude is to objects, events or other individuals in their immediate locality (turning up their noses at an unpleasant smell, for instance, or smiling when a friend enters the room); they can respond with a steady flow of visual feedback, positive or negative, to activities and conversations going on around them (making intermittent eye contact with whoever is holding the floor to indicate that they are attending; looking ostentatiously away when a speaker is trying to engage their attention to indicate boredom or dislike; squeezing their face into an interested or alert expression, or raising their eyes to heaven in a face-threatening display of indifference or disbelief). If they are the speaker, they can make use of similar sets of kinesic cues to manage turn-taking during conversation: indicating by means of a head movement or eye contact that they are willing to cede the floor (Levinson, 1983: 302), perhaps to a specific targeted individual, or avoiding such behaviours precisely as a means of prolonging their conversational turn. Verbal behaviour of various kinds can also come into play: participants who know they can be heard by co-present others can choose to produce a range of 'back-channel' cues (Goffman, 1981: 14) to indicate conversational support ('uh-huh', 'then what?'); once they are themselves in possession of the floor they can select the next turn-taker via a direct address to some or all of those co-present (consider that staple of the seminar situation, 'what do *the rest of you* think?', uttered by a tutor to the seminar group at large, often when one participant has been dominating the discussion). In a shared locale, prosodic cues, too, have their part to play: an increased speech rate or louder voice will drown out someone who is trying to interrupt; particular intonation patterns can be used to indicate the speaker's affective orientation towards their own contribution (surprise; amusement; grief; fury ...); paralinguistic features such as particular tones of voice can indicate to familiars that the speaker wishes their utterance to be taken ironically, or at face value, or with a pinch of salt. Taken together, in face-to-face encounters prosodic, kinesic and linguistic cues can function to structure interactions and to deliver a range of expressive signals, contextualizing what is said and permitting the disambiguation of potentially face-threatening acts. As Thompson puts it:

> Participants in face-to-face interactions are constantly and routinely engaged in comparing the various symbolic cues employed by speakers, using them to reduce ambiguity and to refine their understanding of the message. If participants detect inconsistencies, or cues that do not tally with one another, this can become a source of trouble which may threaten the continuation of the interaction and cast doubt on the sincerity of the speaker.

(Thompson, 1995: 83)

To see and be seen, to hear and be heard also facilitates *dialogue* (Thompson, 1995: 82). While we can easily conjure up a range of face-to-face interactive situations which involve one participant holding the floor in a lengthy monologue (institutional settings such as lecture theatres, classrooms and churches being obvious examples[8]), face-to-face encounters, as the previous paragraphs' brief delineation of turn-taking mechanisms suggests, also allow for a fully bilateral exchange of information in which more than one co-present participant can take the floor successively, responding to remarks made by previous individuals and initiating new topics, monitoring feedback and being monitored in turn. Conversation, 'that familiar predominant kind of talk in which two or more participants freely alternate in speaking' (Levinson, 1983: 284), is always potentially on offer when two or more individuals are in the same place.

1.3   Communicative Affordances

In canonical encounters, *space* (the set of relations between relevant objects and individuals) is fundamentally linked to *place* (the arena in which these relations are structured), so that the relevant physical relationships between conversational participants, and between those participants and the objects around them, are constrained by the boundaries of the locale in which they find themselves. Two or more people in the same place thus loosely share a set of spatial relations to their immediate environment and to each other. If they are in a garden, then a

---

[8] See Scannell (1996: 18ff.) for a discussion of the structural features attendant upon participation in institutional occasions.

tree, say, might loom over all concerned if they are seated beneath it, or will block the sun if they are lying on loungers with the tree overhead. Similarly, if I am watching television with three of my friends then one of them may be on my left, on the second of two sofas which face in the general direction of the television set, and the other two may be on my right, sharing the other sofa with me; the television itself will be broadly 'in front' of all of us, though each individual's spatial orientation to it will be slightly and uniquely different, depending on where they are sitting, whether they are leaning forward or back, whether they are slumped in a position where they are forced to look upwards in order for their gaze to encounter the screen, are alert and upright and gazing directly ahead, or are reaching for another handful of snacks, with their gaze and their primary bodily orientation directed elsewhere in the room.

It is this fundamental association of space with place in the canonical encounter which gives rise to the interactional characteristics that I discussed in the previous section: the ever-present possibility of conversational encounters taking place; the use of deictic expressions, and of gestural deictics in particular, to index elements in the immediate vicinity; and the availability of linguistic, paralinguistic, prosodic and kinesic features which cue co-present listeners as to who is holding the floor, what their communicative intentions are and how they are responding to objects, events and individuals around them. In a situation where space maps onto place, participants can make use of expressions that either index features *of* the environment (*this smell*; *that sound*; *those apples*) or express a spatial relation *to* the environment ('put it *over there*'; 'bring that *here*') with reasonable confidence that their listeners will understand them; the full and extensive use of linguistic, extralinguistic and paralinguistic cues is similarly dependent upon a set of circumstances in which you and I both have at least the potential to be spatially orientated towards each other in the same place.

Such a situation only holds good, of course, if all relevant conversational partners are co-present. In mediated interactions, where one or more participants are physically absent and communicating via an intervening medium rather than through the air in the place in which they jointly find themselves,[9] spatial relations can no longer be contained within a single bounded arena:

> In pre-modern societies, space and place largely coincide, since the spatial dimensions of social life are, for most of the population, and in most respects, dominated by 'presence' – by localised activities. The advent of modernity increasingly tears space away from place by fostering relations between 'absent' others, locationally distant from any given situation of face-to-face interaction.

(Giddens, 1990: 18–19)

---

[9] 'Primarily' is an important word here: face-to-face encounters may involve limited kinds of intervening media, such as the piece of paper used by students in a classroom to exchange scribbled notes with each other, or the megaphone used by speakers to address a crowd at a rally. These will not count as mediated interactions for our purposes here as the definition in 1.2 specifically makes reference to physical absence. Cf. Thompson (1995: 83) who similarly situates the mediated interaction in terms of 'the use of a technical medium … which enables information or symbolic content to be transmitted to individuals who are remote in space, in time, or in both'.

I will return in the next chapter to consider the wider question of modernity which is raised in this quote from Giddens, and to discuss its implications for understanding both space and time in mediated interactions. For the moment, however, I wish to concentrate on the kind of 'dislocation' (Moores, 1997: 238) of space and place which Giddens also broaches here.

This notion of dislocation we can usefully investigate via a further examination of the typology of interactional characteristics which we examined in 1.2, with reference to the extent to which particular electronic media offer the full range of sensory modalities to the embodied individual. This discussion, in turn, will provide a basis for classifying various kinds of remote encounter along a cline stretching from 'thin' at one extreme (encounters with objects which provide only the most limited kind of sensory and/or kinesic access) to relatively 'thick' encounters at the other, where particular media appear to offer the individual a relation to the mediated world which approximates to full co-presence. This will permit us to undertake a functional analysis of the relationship between particular communicative situations and the interactional characteristics that they do or do not facilitate.

The idea of the *communicative affordance* will be of central importance to this discussion. The concept of affordances was originally developed by Gibson (1982), and refers broadly to the way in which the functionality of an object does or does not enable particular kinds of actions on the part of an individual engaging with it. Hutchby (2001: 26) takes up and expands upon this idea to talk about the notion of the *communicative* affordance, the 'possibilities for action that emerge from ... given technological forms' (Hutchby, 2001: 30). The concept of communicative affordances has already implicitly permeated the discussion in this chapter. To talk about the range of interactive structures and behaviours that are characteristic of the canonical situation is to talk about the communicative affordances of face-to-face engagements, about the kinds of encounters that they allow or disallow.

The notion of communicative affordances, as Hutchby is at some pains to point out, is not technologically deterministic. Although a particular form or medium may proscribe certain kinds of behaviour and seemingly prescribe others, users may choose not to interact with it in the anticipated way. As an example of the manner in which technological forms may be appropriated for purposes other than those originally intended, Hutchby cites Grint and Woolgar on the development of telephone technology:

> [T]elephone technology was used originally to broadcast concert music. It was not axiomatic to its design that the telephone system would ultimately be restricted primarily to two-way personal communication ... The original use of telephone technology, and indeed its use now, was and is the result of interpretation and negotiations, not determinations.

(Grint and Woolgar, 1997: 21, cited in Hutchby, 2001: 21)

Conversely, we can consider the early arguments around the appropriate uses of radio technology, which 'was first conceived as a means of point-to-point communication' (Peters, 1999: 206), but where the inherently public and unconstrainable nature of the signal aroused anxieties concerning the privacy of communication, leading to its eventual manifestation as a broadcast medium decades later. Radio waves, as Peters (1999: 195) points out, can potentially be used either as 'a central exchange for many voices' (radio broadcasting) or as 'a means for point-to-point contact' (ham radio); the same holds true for telephone technology (party lines on the one hand; mobile phones on the other). That the one developed primarily for interpersonal communication and the other for broadcast has to do with a dialectic between the communicative affordances of each form on the one hand and the history of its contexts of appropriation on the other.

The developers, manufacturers and managers of particular technological forms, in other words, cannot altogether prescribe what their equipment will be used for. Nor can they control the kinds of behaviours which will accompany its use. Peters, for example, notes the entertaining comments of one American journalist concerning the audience's lack of listening decorum:

> Bruce Bliven noted in 1924 that most political orators, if aware of 'the ribald comments addressed to the stoical loud-speaker' of the home-receiver, would seek other jobs. 'The comments of the family range from Bill's "Is *that* so!" down to Howard's irreverent "Aw, shut your face, you poor hunk of cheese!"' Home listening allowed oratory to be received in a mood of chronic flippancy.

> (Peters, 1999: 213)

The array of uses to which a particular form will be put, then, cannot be entirely anticipated or controlled; nor can the range of attendant behaviours. We should not, however, allow the anti-deterministic thrust of the argument to blind us to what will be the central issue for the rest of this chapter. If particular forms can give rise to unintended uses and/or modes of reception, it is nevertheless part and parcel of the communicative affordances of any given form or medium that there are certain activities which it *disenables*, which it does not allow the user to pursue.

We can take as an initial starting point here Peters' contention that there are certain sense faculties that are not amenable to communication at a distance:

> Of all the senses, touch is the most resistant to being made into a medium of recording or transmission. It remains stubbornly wed to the proximate; indeed, with taste, it is the only one sense that has no remote capacity ... Touch defies inscription rather more than seeing or hearing.

> (Peters, 1999: 269)

Why should it be the case that the objects of touch and taste – and smell, for that matter – cannot be accessed via a remote encounter? The short answer is that all three are faculties that depend for their functioning upon an immediate and corporeal interaction with the world. To taste something, our tongues must physically engage with it; to touch, our hands or bodies must do so; to smell, we must be in the immediate vicinity of the olfactory object; and self-evidently, we cannot employ tongues, hands, noses or our own bodies at a distance from ourselves. As Merleau-Ponty (1962: 316) puts it, 'Tactile experience ... adheres to the surface of our body'. Vision, he adds, 'presents us with a spectacle spread out before us at a distance, and gives us the illusion of being immediately present everywhere and being situated nowhere' (Merleau-Ponty, 1962: 316); the same would seem to hold true of hearing. On the face of it, therefore, no medium will be able to afford us access to touch or taste or smell at a distance because each of these requires immediate proximity in order to operate.

But if part of the answer relates to the ways in which our sense faculties function, then another important element has to do with the question of communicative affordances. We cannot see or hear anything beyond our immediate vicinity either: once something is too far away for me to see it, or out of the range of my hearing, then I will not have direct access to what it looks or sounds like any more than I will to its touch or taste. When we listen to a voice on the telephone or interact with a friend over a video-conferencing link we do not reach directly into their remote location by some species of teleperception (eyes or ears on stalks); rather, we engage, *where we are*, with a *representation*, a filtered and transformed variant of the thing: a voice on the phone which sounds sultrier than it is because of the suppression of high frequencies (Peters, 1999: 196); a video-conferenced homunculus on our computer screen which is pixilated and out-of-sync with the words it is speaking. Even if the image on the screen were to be maximally high-resolution, or the voice on the phone were indistinguishable from the unique vocal qualities of a particular individual, though, we would still be encountering a representation: we cannot remotely encounter the real.[10]

It is the 'technical forms' that Hutchby talks about which deliver these representations to us: projectors, telephones, computers, televisions, radios, VCRs, DVD players and the like. Hence the difficulty as far as taste, touch and smell are concerned. Even if we were prepared to lick or paw the apparatus to achieve gratification, thus overcoming the problem of proximity, nothing could be oozing out of it to meet us. Taste or touch do not simply require immediate contact, but immediate contact with an appropriate perceptual object. The apparatus would have to transmit something that we could lick or paw in the first place, and it is entirely unclear what species of medium would permit the transmission of the kind of three-dimensional entities that we would need to directly engage with in order to touch or taste them. We could, it is true, get hold of a card from a television station which would permit us to lick particular squares in order to approximate to the taste of a food just then being consumed on the television screen; the ill-fated experiments with scratch'n'sniff cards in cinemas spring to mind here. But an encounter with a scratch'n'sniff card is in principle no different from the individual who sniffs their beloved's letter, hoping to find a trace of their perfume on it. Such an encounter does not transmit to us, *from a distance*, something that we could smell, but only allows us to engage, *where we are*, with the piece of card or paper that the scent is imprinted on. It is possible, of course, to consider the Proustian case where a representation interacts with memory in such a way as to cause us to have something akin to

---

[10]Whether we can directly encounter the real under any circumstances is a question that is beyond the scope of this book; but see Chapter 5 for a further discussion of this matter.

a momentary apperception of a similar object which we have encountered in another time and another place; such an apperception, though, does not deliver the perceptual object itself to the *place where we are* but only reminds us of what it felt like to encounter it elsewhere. It is also, perhaps, possible to imagine a technological form which could waft odours for us to encounter in the privacy of our own room at dramatically appropriate moments, making the sense of smell a kind of intermediate category in this discussion. Were such an apparatus to teleport 3D objects for us to touch or taste, however, then those objects would inevitably, once teleported, be local rather than remote: although they would be coming at us from afar, we would encounter them face-to-face.

1.4 The Mediated Encounter

With touch and taste – and to a considerable extent, smell – taken out of the equation, we are left with just four of Avery and McCain's seven sensory modalities to consider: the audio verbal, the audio non-verbal, the visual verbal and the visual pictorial. Only the faculties of sight and sound, in other words, have the potential to be engaged when we interact remotely with the world. The sense of touch, it should be noted, will not re-enter the picture even in the case of written communication. It is, of course, perfectly possible for an individual in receipt of a missive from the beloved not only to sniff the piece of paper but to touch it and perhaps even to rustle it as well as actually reading the contents. This scenario suggests an encounter with the medium which seems little short of the thickness of actual co-presence, with sight, sound, smell and touch all entering the equation; but this approach is fundamentally flawed. It is not the encounter with the *medium* which will be of relevance here, but the encounter with the absent individual or individuals which the medium affords. The example of the letter suggests the thickness of co-presence because co-presence (of the recipient with the letter) is the actual state of affairs.

If it is the case, then, that the only sense faculties that remote encounters permit us to bring into play are the auditory and the visual, then it immediately becomes clear that no mediated encounter is going to be able to deliver anything other than a relatively thin engagement with the world. This conclusion is entirely in keeping with the argument developed earlier in this chapter. If, as Merleau-Ponty argues, it is only in full co-existence with a phenomenon that we can be said to comprehensively engage with it (Merleau-Ponty, 1962: 318), then remote encounters, with their fundamentally restricted access to the range of sense modalities on offer in the canonical situation, will be able to bring the world to us only in the flat slices that are all that remain after the majority of information has been cut away.

What, though, does this discussion have to tell us about the affordances of different electronic media of communication, as far as encounters with absent others are concerned? Thompson, in his account of mediated encounters, draws a distinction between three types of interaction: face-to-face interactions, mediated interactions and what he refers to as the 'mediated quasi-interaction'

(Thompson, 1995: 82). Four characteristics are used to define these categories: whether they involve a local or a remote encounter; whether the communication is aimed at specific or non-specific others; the dialogical or monological affordances of the situation; and the range of symbolic cues which they do or do not afford participants (1995: 85). The example of the letter which we have been exploring here, for instance, would constitute, in Thompson's terms, a remote encounter (the recipient is in another place at another time) with a specific other, which is potentially dialogical in nature (the recipient can write back), and has a particular and limited range of symbolic cues on offer, and thus for Thompson, the letter would count as a *mediated interaction*. These are characterized by the dislocation of space and place; the limited availability of symbolic cues; an orientation towards a specific other or others; and the potential for a bilateral encounter. As a more detailed example of this category we can consider video-conferencing.

Both sight and sound – the two faculties that we have left at our disposal – would appear at first glance to be readily facilitated during video-conferencing. I can see, on my computer screen, the remote individual I am interacting with, and I can presume that they can similarly, in their own context of co-presence, see me; and I will be able to make a similar assumption about our mutual ability to hear each other.

Video-conferencing, by this description, should thus afford individuals the range of interactive structures and behaviours that characterize the canonical encounter, as these are primarily dependent upon an ability to see and hear fellow participants. At first glance, this would appear to cast doubt on Thompson's assertion that mediated encounters involve a restricted range of cues. In a situation where you and I believe ourselves to be simultaneously audible and visible to each other we can certainly engage in dialogue; and many of the other features I discussed in 1.2 would seem to be equally accessible. Gestural deictics, for example, which depend for their felicitous use on my hearer being able to monitor my indexical behaviour, seem to be warranted by a situation where my hearer can see me; ditto, the use of the array of linguistic, paralinguistic and kinesic cues which permit the two of us to structure the interaction and convey an assortment of affective states and responses. Just as in the canonical encounter, I appear to be able to presuppose that my listener, if they know me well enough, will be able to have a crack at decoding paralinguistic features of my utterance in order to recognize that I am intending to be taken ironically when I say, from Glasgow, 'it's a lovely day again here'; will recognize that particular kinds of vocatives are intended to elicit a response from them and thus to pass them the floor ('what's the weather like there, Jane?'); will appreciate that my intermittent uttering of back-channel cues ('wow, really?') indicates that I am attending to and gripped by their contribution, and so on. We appear, in other words, to be able to engage in conversation, with the full range of resources available to us.

The above discussion needs to be qualified in a number of ways, however. The webcam that relays my image to an absent other can take in only a certain amount of my immediate environment, generally centred around my face and upper body; and whilst I can indeed use gestural deictics, my use will be constrained by what I can hold up to the webcam or can reasonably assume to be sufficiently proximate to fall within its visual range. I cannot conceivably indicate objects that are behind the computer – a picture on the wall, say – unless I swivel the webcam round and cease temporarily to be within the frame of my own interaction. This kind of remote encounter, in other words, does not afford participants the kind of 360 degree access to the perceptual field which they can readily obtain in a canonical encounter. There will likely be similar restrictions governing your ability to *hear* what is going on in my vicinity. You will almost certainly have access to my voice; but depending on the quality of the microphone, I may or may not be able to felicitously draw your attention to the sound of the telephone ringing in the next room by saying 'hang on, I have to answer *that*'.

Further difficulties abound. I have already noted the reduced and pixilated representation of the individual which video-conferencing affords. Hutchby adds to this list of potential drawbacks the issue of download speed:

> Even the most powerful desktop computers have trouble displaying real-time internet video at a data transfer rate sufficient to eliminate observable jerkiness and 'frame-dropping', largely because of internet bandwidth restrictions. This is the case even with images displayed in a box only a couple of inches square. Attempts at a full-screen resolution result in a 'blocky' image in which the nuances of phenomena such as gaze direction and facial expression are easily lost.

> (Hutchby, 2001: 124)

Hutchby notes, too, a further relevant phenomenon. The webcams which permit us to see remote others are not embedded in the computer screen, but are elsewhere, generally on top of the computer monitor (2001: 127). In order to see you, I need to focus my gaze on the window in my screen where your image is available; if I do so, however, then I will not appear to you to be meeting your gaze, for which I need instead to be directing my gaze to the webcam that captures my image for you. To you, my direct gaze at your image on my screen, which represents for me the intimacy of eye contact, will appear as a gaze downwards. Video-conferencing would therefore appear to rule out the possibility of a mutual gaze: for me to appear to you to be making eye contact, I need to be looking into the webcam, in which case I cannot look to see whether you are making eye contact with me.

This combination of circumstances has a number of implications for the degree to which video-conferencing affords its participants the full array of interactive behaviours. As the quote from Hutchby makes clear, facial expressions cannot be reliably used to convey feedback to my speaker, although as a user of the technology I may of course be unaware of this and may be happily contorting my face in a variety of elaborative gestures which cannot be recognized in the window on your screen in which I am currently manifesting myself. Kinesic cues such as head movements to indicate that I am offering you the floor may also be hard to read given the resolution of the image; and the use of gaze for similar ends will be destined, of course, to fail, given the asymmetry of gaze which the situation as it is currently constituted affords. This particular technology, in other words, does indeed restrict the range of cues, both symbolic and otherwise, which a participant can provide for the absent other they are addressing.

Thompson contrasts his category of mediated interaction with what he refers to as *mediated quasi-interactions*. Whilst the latter also involve Thompson's 'separation of contexts' (1995: 85) and a limited set of symbolic cues, they are distinguished by being aimed at an indefinite range of participants and by being fundamentally monological in character. What Thompson has in mind is 'the kinds of social relations established by the media of mass communication (books, newspapers, radio, television, etc.)' (Thompson, 1995: 84). We can take as an example here television's address to the audience at home. Video-conferencing offers its participants the possibility of seeing and hearing along a single pathway: a bi-directional vector stretching from my machine to yours and back again for as long as we are both connected to the internet and the relevant software is running. Television, like video-conferencing, involves the faculties of sight and sound; but the sensory modalities that can be accessed – the audio verbal, the audio non-verbal, the visual verbal and the visual pictorial – are typically said to be asymmetrically available. When I watch television, I can see what there is to be seen on the screen, and hear what is coming out of my speakers, but I can be neither heard nor seen at the other end. If I am watching and listening to an individual on my screen, then, I cannot directly respond, or so the argument goes: unlike video-conferencing, this individual will have no access to my own context of co-presence, and is therefore functionally blind and deaf as far as any communications on my part are concerned. I can see and hear, but not speak; the other, on the screen, can speak but cannot see or hear me.

What are the consequences of this asymmetrical communicative situation? Television performers, for their part, can felicitously carry out many of the activities and behaviours that are associated with face-to-face communication. Just as gestural deictics can be used by either participant in a video-conferencing transaction, so they can be used by the television performer to index elements in their immediate vicinity. The television chef, for instance, can clearly indicate items of food, cooking paraphernalia and the like via a gesture and a demonstrative expression (*'this* is what we'll be preparing today'), secure in the assumption that anyone at home paying attention will be able to determine the appropriate object because they will be able to see the relevant gestures. Individuals on television can, too, make use of particular tones of voice to mark their utterance as ironic or deadly serious; and can indicate via their intonation that they are angry, or neutral, or amazed.

What they cannot typically do, however, on this view, is to make use of some of the interactive mechanisms that characterize a dialogical exchange. Those interactive mechanisms that have to do with *addressing* relevant conversational participants are still available: the gaze to the webcam can be replaced by a gaze to camera, and direct address of a non-specific kind ('on today's programme *you're* going to see') can clearly operate felicitously in a situation where they can be seen and heard by absent others. Performers cannot, however, offer the viewer the floor; nor would there be any point in them producing back-channel cues, as there is no flow of information from the viewer for them to respond to or support.

On this view, television's affordances are thus clearly different, characteristically, from the affordances of the internet, with its potential for symmetrical communication. We can typically rule out conversation, for a start, which requires a two-way flow of information: even though, as the earlier quote from Peters suggests, viewers can rail and shake their fists at the screen when they do not like what they are watching, the performer at the other end will be blissfully unaware. There is no point in their using gestural deictics, nor indeed is there any point in their having recourse to any of the behaviours that would allow them to interact with the other: they are invisible and inaudible, and cannot communicate with the individual who is addressing them.

This kind of 'mediated quasi-interaction', however, with its absence of one-on-one communication and its preclusion of a direct response on the part of the viewer or listener comprises only one of many possible 'communicative circuits' (Scannell, 1991: 11) in play in broadcast communication. There are a number of routes through which individual members of the remote audience can enter into a bilateral encounter with a performer on television. Other media of electronic communication such as the telephone, for example, can be used to text or to speak directly with someone on the television; and there is, too, the example of the kind of live television programme where cameras are set up in remote locations in such a way that members of the audience can be momentarily seen and heard on the screen.[11] For this reason, in what follows, I will continue to use the term 'mediated encounter' to cover all instances of televisual interaction-at-a-distance. Whilst television, in its address to its audience, clearly and routinely constructs a different set of affordances from those available to someone engaged in a two-way internet transaction, it also affords other modes of engagement, less asymmetrical in form.

There is another reason, too, for maintaining a single overarching category of the mediated encounter in what follows. This chapter has argued that the interactional structures and behaviours which can arise in particular kinds of communicative situations are directly consequent upon the nature of the context of utterance. Thompson's account does not dispute this. He stresses, for instance, that his category of 'mediated interaction' is stretched across time and space and 'thereby acquires a number of characteristics which differentiate it from face-to-face interaction' (Thompson, 1995: 83); indeed his project is bound up with tracing the social and interactional consequences of the forms of communication characteristic of modernity. Where the two arguments might diverge, however, is in the emphasis which will be placed here on the affordances of particular media of communication, on what they will or will not allow individuals to do. Where Thompson wishes to distinguish mediated quasi-interactions from mediated interactions on the basis of the particular communicative circuit in operation and its implications for dialogical communication, the fundamentally *phenomenological* investigation in this chapter would lead us, rather, to consider such encounters as a routinized consequence of broadcasting's affordances to

---

[11] On the role of other forms of electronic communication in constructing an interactive channel, see Chapter 7; on live television and the articulation of different places, see Chapter 6.

its users. The electronic broadcasting media allow individuals to be seen and heard at a distance via the microphone, the camera and a variety of methods of broadcast transmission (cables, satellites, terrestrial signals) but not to see or hear through these particular artefacts; a one-way address to absent others would seem to be an obvious entailment of this particular set of circumstances, although the capacities of users to transcend the limitations of a particular form or medium are not to be underestimated, as we shall see in due course.

1.5   Conclusion

I began this chapter by saying that mediated encounters and face-to-face interactions are significantly different from each other. We have now seen at least some of the reasons why this is the case. In a context of co-presence, space maps onto place, and co-present individuals will thus share, subject to their precise orientation, a roughly equivalent set of spatial relations to the objects around them. To be present in a particular place, furthermore, affords individuals access to the full range of sensory modalities on offer. All participants, to the extent that they are in full possession of their senses, will therefore be able to smell, touch, taste, hear and see the same objects. Taken together, these properties of the canonical encounter mean that individuals can identify and locate a range of phenomena with a reasonable degree of security that the objects and individuals they indicate will be identifiable to those around them, and can make use of a full range of prosodic, kinesic and linguistic cues to engage with each other.

In mediated encounters, by contrast, individuals do not inhabit the same context of co-presence. This dislocation of space from place means that they no longer share a spatial orientation to the set of objects in each vicinity. Nor can they touch or taste (or, very likely, smell) the same phenomena; and to the extent that they can see or hear what is going on elsewhere, this is by virtue of a locally available representation only, with all that that entails in terms of image or sound quality. As a consequence, mediated encounters effect a 'narrowing' (Thompson, 1995: 85) of the available range of conversational cues, and may also involve restrictions in the use of certain kinds of context-dependent language such as deictic expressions. Under certain circumstances, furthermore, mediated encounters will only permit asymmetrical encounters, where one or more participants will be unable to interact directly with others.

Mediated interactions may, however, possess a range of mechanisms to compensate for the lost functionalities of the canonical encounter, and it would be a mistake to view them simply in terms of what they lack in comparison to face-to-face encounters. Whilst certain kinds of interactive machinery will not work because of the restricted access to relevant conversational participants which a particular technological form or medium may afford, other mechanisms will exist, or will be developed, which will allow users to overcome with varying degrees of success the limitations of the apparatus. Take, for example, the letter that I discussed earlier. The writer cannot make use of prosodic cues to orient the recipient to the import of the communication, but can, for instance, use underlining or CAPITALS expressively, and has the option of communicating via graphic cues as well (little hearts, kisses and a variety of affectionate squiggles). As Thompson puts it:

> Communication by means of letters ... deprives the participants of a range of cues associated with physical co-presence (gestures, facial expressions, intonation, etc.) while other symbolic cues are accentuated.

(Thompson, 1995: 83)

Or take the example of deictic expressions. We might well expect it to be the case that gestural deictics cannot be used felicitously in written communication, as they depend for their interpretation on other participants being able to monitor the speaker's indexical behaviour. It ought, then, to be the case that I cannot, in a letter or email, expect my recipient to make sense of what I am saying if I ask them to 'look at this', or indeed if I enquire whether my 'bum looks big in this'. This is not, however, entirely the case. An arrow, indexing a drawing in a letter or a photograph in an email, will serve just as well as a physical gesture; similarly, we would have no trouble making sense of a button on a website which urged us to 'press here'. Just as pictorial cues in letters (and the offline or online use of emoticons in computer-mediated communications) permit the writer to add affective overtones of various kinds to what they are saying, so graphic information can be used indexically, in place of the physical indexical behaviour of a co-present participant, to pick out particular features of the environment.

Nor should we necessarily think of these mechanisms invariably as compensatory, as a way of overcoming specific interactional problems entailed by the thinness of remote encounters. This would be to inappropriately privilege the canonical encounter, and although the argument in this chapter takes the canonical situation as ontologically prior (as Thompson (1995: 81) puts it, 'For most of human history, most forms of social interaction have been face-to-face') it is nevertheless clear that more historically recent forms of communication-at-a-distance do not simply seek to mimic the patterns and structures of face-to-face interaction but may in some cases complement or supplant them. The affordances of an apparatus that delivers a remote encounter may be additive as well as subtractive, in other words; and while I will have reason to argue that there may be pressing reasons why particular media of communication might wish to develop mechanisms to simulate the immediacy of the face-to-face encounter, it is also the case that the absence of certain functionalities in certain situations may be a positive advantage. The letter, after all, may be designed to end a relationship in a way which avoids the intimacy and emotional commitment of a face-to-face encounter: the writer may precisely wish to avoid monitoring the recipient's feedback. We can cite also in this respect Hutchby's analysis of internet relay chat, which affords certain possibilities for conversational turn-taking, such as nominating the individual at whom the writer wishes to target their utterance ('allo Nicky'; 'you got a pic then zazoo') but where the interactive free-for-all constituted by a multiplicity of participants all potentially typing messages at the same time can also be, in Hutchby's terms 'serendipitous' (Hutchby, 2001: 191), creating ambiguities in turn-taking and address which permit participants a wider freedom to interact with unknown others than they would have in a face-to-face situation where kinesic, linguistic and prosodic cues would likely function to circumscribe the interaction.

All mediated encounters, furthermore, self-evidently afford their users one incalculable advantage over individuals interacting in a canonical situation. Whilst, as we have seen, mediated encounters are perilously thin in terms of their ability to deliver to remote participants the full range of sense objects thus imposing particular kinds of limitations on the way in which interactive tokens can be displayed, it is nevertheless the case that mediated encounters allow us to engage with others *at a distance*, to stretch our communications across space. Seen from this perspective, it is the canonical encounter which comes to look limited, with its narrow and singular perceptual field and the constraints it imposes upon participants' ability to jointly transcend space in their transactions with each other. To truly get a handle on the extraordinary nature of these taken-for-granted encounters-at-a-distance which now routinely permeate our contexts of co-presence, though, it is necessary to think not only about matters of space and place but also about the related question of *time*. This I will proceed to do in the next chapter, where we will start once more from first principles in order to examine the impact of mediated communication on individuals' experience of the world at the moment in which they encounter it.

2

Time, Space and Electronic Communication

2.1 The Immediate Vicinity

In a garden in the late 1940s, the phenomenologist Alfred Schutz is working on the first chapter of his study *Reflections on the Problem of Relevance*. His opening paragraph graphically captures for the reader his sensory and kinaesthetic engagement with his immediate vicinity, with all of its myriad aspects and textures:

> Having decided to jot down some thoughts on the matter of relevance, I have arranged my writing materials on a table in the garden of my summer house. Starting the first strokes of my pen, I have in my visual field this white sheet of paper, my writing hand, the ink marks forming one line of characters after the other on the white background. Before me is the table with its green surface on which several objects are placed – my pencil, two books, and other things. Further on are the trees and lawns of my garden, the lake with boats, the mountain, and the clouds in the background. I need only turn my head to see the house with its porch, the windows of my room, etc. I hear the buzzing of a motorboat, the voices of the children in the neighbour's yard, the calling of the bird. I experience the kinesthetic movements of my writing hand, I have sensations of warmth. I feel the table supporting my writing arm. All of this is within my perceptual field, a field well organized into spheres of objects: those within my reach, those which once have been within my reach and can be brought within it again, and those which thus far have never been within my reach but which I may bring within it by means of appropriate kinesthetic movements of particular kinds.

> (Schutz, 1970: 1)

In a few brief sentences here, Schutz offers us an arresting account of the immediacy of co-presence. He will go on to make the point that none of the elements around him will be horizonal (1970: 4) or thematic for him in what follows; he has other fish to fry. Nevertheless, for the moments in which he is penning the paragraph we are offered all the intensity of an individual's focused engagement with their immediate environment, with its full access to the range of sensory modalities on offer.

For a reader encountering this paragraph more than half a century later, what may be most striking about the writer's environment is the items and experiences which are lacking. The sounds that Schutz acquaints us with do not include a telephone ringing, or music or voices from a radio or television. Similarly, the 'kinesthetic movements' which he experiences as he produces these words come from his 'writing hand', and not from a two-handed tapping on the keyboard of a laptop or the manipulation of its mouse.

The absence of these artefacts walls Schutz off from all forms of immediate interruption bar one. If we wished to communicate with him in real time – having somehow transported ourselves back to the appropriate moment – then we would need to turn up at his house, go into the garden and become part of the immediate vicinity with which he can interact. The mobile technologies which would permit him to have amongst the 'other things' on his table a mobile phone, pager, radio, PDA portable television or laptop have not yet been developed, and so we cannot ring, text, page or email him or send him an instant message. Nor would there be any point in us sending in a request in his name to a radio station or engaging in a television phone-in in the hope that he might be watching.[1] Whilst a number of telecommunications technologies are in place in the late 1940s which would permit individuals to engage instantaneously with distant places – the telegraph, the telephone, the radio, the television – none of them are in the garden.

We would, then, be unable to participate in an immediate interaction with Schutz unless we were actually *there*. If we were to drop in on him then we could – providing he let us in – engage in a face-to-face encounter, in the course of which we too would be free to hear the motorboat and the birds singing and observe the distant line of the mountains, and would be able to converse about all or any of these in the modes that are available to co-present individuals ('listen to *that racket*'; 'I've always meant to climb up *there*'). We would, in other words share – approximately, and for most intents and purposes – the *here-and-now* of his sitting in the garden: the *here* because we would have physically relocated ourselves to where he is, and the *now* because we would share the present moment in which both we and he would be encountering the world. Remove us from the garden – to a point some streets away, say – and we would still co-exist in the same shared present moment, but it would no longer be *operational* from the point of view of communication. Any utterances that we produced, any activities that we engaged in, would be inaccessible to Schutz *at the moment when we generated them*, because they would not be unfolding in a shared perceptual field. He could certainly apprise himself of them later – reading a letter we are currently writing to him once it is delivered tomorrow, for instance – but the absence of electronic forms of communication from his immediate vicinity would rule out the possibility of our interacting with him *now* unless we were physically co-present.

Is Schutz, then, entirely in a world of his own? Not quite. There is, for one thing, the boat on the lake from which we could, as a last resort, semaphore him a message and hope that he is looking in the right direction at the crucial moment. The boat would serve to transfer us from elsewhere into the *here* of Schutz's vicinity, shrinking space – the distance between us – and rendering us part of his here-and-now in the process. The boat could thus be used to bring us – or our message, at least – into his immediate presence. This we could accomplish partly through the act of travelling, rendering what is absent present through movement

---

[1] We could, however, attempt to get someone to broadcast him a message via a crystal radio or foxhole radio, should he have such a thing. Dedicated readers can no doubt come up with other plausible scenarios. See http://members.aol.com/djadamson7/articles/foxhole.html (accessed 1 September 2005) on the construction of foxhole radios by GIs in World War II.

from one place to another; and partly, with the added option of semaphore, through *telecommunication*: communication across distance. Semaphore, in common with other species of pre-electronic communication – drumming, smoke signals, hilltop beacons and the like (Carey, 1989: 203; Kern, 1983: 68) would allow us to exchange and transmit information via serial pairs of instantaneous connections (A signalling to B, B to C and so on), permitting us to communicate messages from somewhere beyond where he could hear what we are saying or read our lips. We should note, however, that if we are part of an elaborate chain of semaphore messages designed to urgently rouse Schutz and direct his attention to something other than what is currently horizonal for him, then the fractional delay between one message-pair and the next will mean that communication from the furthest point to the nearest is not instantaneous.

Both travel and (relatively primitive forms of) telecommunication, then, would allow us to do what we cannot otherwise achieve: to insert ourselves and our own concerns into a non-proximate place. One further artefact, already present in Schutz's immediate vicinity, will achieve similar results, permitting an exchange of information across space and time. Whilst Schutz (semaphoring aside) is safe from the real-time predations of absent others, the 'two books' that he has on his table will still allow him to engage with ideas that come to him from a distance. Printing, like semaphore, is a species of *space-binding* technology (Carey, 1989; Innis, 1951), technology that permits communication across distance. Schutz's books will serve to shrink space, bringing information from *there* into *here* to be consumed at leisure in the *now* of the reader's encounter with it.

This *now* of the reader would, however, inevitably be distinct from the 'generative now' (Husserl, 1964: 45) in which the words were actually written. Schutz's two books will not allow messages to be received in the instant in which they were produced. Time-travel apart, we cannot get back into Schutz's garden to be in the moment in which he is writing: his words come to us across both time and space, and the same is true of the books on his table. There are, as the argument in this section has suggested, only two kinds of situation that will permit participants to engage with each other in the shared *now* of immediate interaction: the canonical or face-to-face situation, in which all participants share roughly the same space-time coordinates, and electronically mediated encounters, with their capacity to transcend both space and time and deliver a message from elsewhere in the instant in which it is generated. The books on Schutz's table fall into neither of these categories; hence the palpable sense of a focused engagement with his immediate vicinity that we encounter when we read his opening paragraph. His is a perfect bubble of co-presence, impermeable to unwarranted interruption for as long as he remains in his garden and bars the gate against intruders.

2.2 Complex Connectivity

Anyone longing for the splendid isolation of the writer in his garden should take heart. We can relatively easily replicate Schutz's situation by leaving the house or the office and taking ourselves off to some local but less-connected spot, divesting ourselves of mobile phones and other accessories before we go. Or we can remove ourselves to some part of the world where the airwaves are relatively free of signals and where fibre optic cables and wi-fi hotspots have yet to manifest themselves. The pace of technological development, after all, does not proceed evenly on a global scale, and it is clearly not the case that all parts of the world have equal access to the technologies of communication that permit distant individuals to interact instantaneously with each other (Massey, 1993: 61; Nowotny, 1994: 10).[2]

To regard the ubiquity of electronic forms of communication (within certain sociocultural arenas at least) simply as some kind of fall from the prelapsarian paradise of Schutz's garden, though, is to arrest ourselves at the level of the taken-for-granted. What we are in danger of overlooking is the extraordinary phenomenological complexity which electronically mediated interactions effect for our encounters with others across space and time. Whilst it is true that Schutz cannot easily be pestered, beleaguered, harassed or annoyed in his garden by any of the two billion or so individuals who co-inhabit the *now* of his putting pen to paper, neither can he access the webs of 'complex connectivity', the 'ever-densening network of interconnections and interdependences' (Tomlinson, 1999: 2) to which electronic forms of communication would admit him. Although he can go into the house and interact instantaneously with an absent other by telephone (always supposing that his summer house possesses such an object) or, once there, can switch on a radio or television to acquaint himself with a drama that is being acted out elsewhere in the real time of his attending to it, the freeze frame that has him in his garden at his table will, as we have seen, permit none of these. He can interact, in his garden, only with those elements which are part of his perceptual field, or alternatively with the stock of experiences of other places and other times which he can retrieve from his memory (Schutz, 1970: 2); he cannot, in the *now* of his encounter with the world, finger the fabric of a distant place through a simple act of connection.

For Schutz in his garden, then seclusion entails an isolation which sets the limits of what can be physically experienced at the boundaries of perceptual awareness. Only what is in his immediate vicinity – within the bounds of his perceptual field – can be heard, seen, smelled, touched or tasted. Moving through space, as we have seen, will alter the set of objects that fall within this perceptual field, so that he can walk into the house or out into the street and encounter another individual, or another individual can walk into the garden and render themselves perceptually available in the process. By entering the garden, I become co-present, sharing (more or less) Schutz's immediate vicinity, with all the communicative consequences which that entails. Electronic forms of communication, however, do more: they permit me to import, temporarily, the localities of others into my own immediate environment without the necessity of being physically present in the place where those individuals are encountering the world. The bounds of my perceptual field become infinitely permeable, open to a multiplicity of interactive

---

[2]Lack of wealth might also grant us an exit point: as Ferguson (1990: 159) points out, the ownership and consumption of personal portable communication systems is a function of affluence.

possibilities which do not require me to transport myself into the *there* of another, or the other to enter physically into the place where I am.

This capacity of electronic communication to render the distant proximate – to bring what is beyond the boundaries of my perceptual field into my immediate vicinity – is dependent on two interrelated factors. The first of these has to do with speed of transmission. Electronic forms of communication are *instantaneous* or near-instantaneous. When I speak to someone on the telephone, or listen to the radio or participate in an internet chatroom (server and bandwidth permitting), I receive the message in the instant or almost in the instant in which it is transmitted, so that I am interacting with some element of the world almost in the same moment as that element is interacting with me.[3] This instantaneity is a communicative affordance of the apparatus I am using, inasmuch as instantaneous communication-at-a-distance is only available to me if I choose to engage with a mechanism that affords it.

Machines could not, however, deliver instantaneity were the world not the way it is and were we not to experience it the way we do. Instantaneity – coincidence of transmission and reception – is predicated, in turn, on *simultaneity*. Put simply, all localities co-exist in the same present moment; *all elsewheres are at once*. In order to grasp the consequences of this for instantaneous electronic encounters, we need to consider the way in which time, space and place collide in an individual's immediate vicinity or locality.

We can note, first, that the world is full of vicinities. If I sit next to someone on a train, then our respective vicinities – our immediate environments, bounded by the limits of our individual perceptual fields – will map almost perfectly onto each other, though one of us may see a little more of a particular slice of the countryside by virtue of sitting by the window, and what is horizonal for each of us will almost certainly be different unless a salient event in our joint perceptual fields is sufficiently arresting to grab the attention of both of us at once.[4] If the train pulls into a station then my own perceptual field will momentarily share a number of elements with the vicinities of various individuals on the platform: the train itself, the sounds of the station, the aroma of fast-food in the station cafe when the door to the carriage is opened. If I am in a flat or apartment, then the vicinity of the individual living above or next door to me may overlap momentarily with mine if they play their music loud enough for it to penetrate through walls or floors and thus temporarily intrude upon me.

The vast majority of vicinities, however, are non-contiguous: their boundaries do not overlap. My friend who is currently on the other side of the city, my

---

[3] With some exceptions. Computer-mediated communication, for example, may involve a time delay because a message sent to me will be affected not only by its upload speed (whether my friend has a phone modem or broadband, and what their bandwidth is) but also by how busy the relevant servers are; and individuals may, of course, choose to interpose some form of time-delay device such as an answerphone for telephone messages.

[4] Cf. Atkinson and Griffiths (1973: 41), who define a vicinity as 'a set of points surrounding and contained within the interior and fabric of an entity ... bounded either by a roughly spherical envelope centred on the entity or by some humanly accepted line of demarcation such as a wall or a political boundary'.

husband who is on vacation several hundred miles away, my sister, still asleep on another continent, have each one of them their own contexts of co-presence, vicinities that are not currently overlapping with each other's or with mine. The same is true of the billions of other people on the planet. Each of them has their own shifting context of co-presence which will never abut my own unless we chance to collide with each other at some point with our respective vicinities in tow.

These multiple vicinities are further differentiated from each other by a number of temporal factors. Some of these have to do with the standardized time of clocks and calendars, others with the cyclical time of seasons, others with personal time. It is 9.30 in the morning where I am, but only 4.30 a.m. for my sister; five months since my last birthday but only a day since my sister's; a working day for me, but not for my husband; summer where I am, but winter in Australia; Saturday morning for me, Friday night in Polynesia. Each of these factors will have entailments for individual or shared localities. It is light where I am, but dark where my sister is. My sister's vicinity may contain objects such as birthday cards or discarded wrapping paper; mine, unless I am particularly determined to hang on to the relevant paraphernalia, will not. My computer keyboard is currently within reach, and has now become momentarily horizonal by the act of writing about it; my husband, on holiday, is more likely to be snoozing or reading the morning paper, whilst in Polynesia they may still be partying. Whilst an umbrella will almost certainly be thematic for me at some point today in Glasgow in the summer, finally, it may be less likely to be so in parts of Australia in the winter.

Other ways of conceptualizing time also enter this equation. Adam (1990: 30) draws a distinction between 'time in events' and 'events in time'. A similar duality is found in Gale's distinction between 'static' and 'dynamic' ways of talking about time (Lyons, 1977: 688), and in McTaggart's (1927) 'B series' and 'A series'. In the B series – Gale's 'static' time, Adam's 'time in events' – time is organized in a linear fashion, with one event following on from or preceding another. These events occur in a fixed order, which is not subject to change and which is independent of the observer's viewpoint:

> [T]ime, in which all things come to be and pass away, necessarily involves a static order or structure … The very same events which are continually changing in respect to their pastness, presentness or futurity are laid out in a permanent order whose generating relation is that of *earlier than*. This is the static or tenseless way of conceiving time, in which the totality of history is viewed in a God-like manner, all events being given at once in a *nunc stans*.
>
> (Gale, 1968: 7)

Seen from this static or 'tenseless' viewpoint, my older sister was born earlier than me, and I was born later; furthermore, my birthday fell earlier this year than hers, as I was born in April and she was born in August. These events – dates of birth, birthdays – will remain ordered in this way whether I am thinking about them today, five years ago or sometime in the future, because their ordering has nothing to do with *when* I think about them, and would thus appear in some fundamental sense to be objectively given.

This static conception of time will not be of central concern in what follows, but the dynamic or 'tensed' way of thinking about time – McTaggart's A series – will. The A series involves the relations of past, present and future, the 'series of positions which run from the far past through the near past to the present, and then from the present through the near future to the far future, or conversely' (McTaggart, 1927: 10). In contrast to what happens in the B series, events in this 'dynamic' time are subject to change: as new events occur, the relation of other events to the present will have shifted, those which were located at the present now being past, and those which were in the future now being present. Viewed from the perspective of dynamic time, it was my sister's birthday *yesterday* and mine some *four months ago*, because I am locating events relative to my own situation at the temporal zero-point. The location of events in time, measured in this way, will change as time goes by, so that *in a month's time* (another dynamic-time statement) my sister's birthday will have been a month ago, and mine will be five months past, because the temporal zero-point will have shifted a month into the future. Dynamic time is thus deictic (Miller and Johnson-Laird, 1976: 417) because it involves the location of events relative to a temporal zero-point centred on an individual. Just as spatial deictics such as *here* and *there*, *this place* and *that place* are used to indicate physical locations with reference to the spatial zero-point which is *where I am*, so temporal deictics such as *today*, *yesterday*, *tomorrow*, *now*, *then*, *this week*, *next week* and *a month ago* are all used to identify moments or intervals of time with respect to the present moment in which I am encountering the world.

In what follows, I will refer to this present moment as the *phenomenological now*. Pre-reflexively and *pre-phenomenally* (Husserl, 1964) no such determinate moment exists; we might rather want to think about the world as 'a continuity of becoming' (Bergson, 1988: 139) in which reality is 'a ceaseless upspringing of something new, which has no sooner arisen to make the present than it has already fallen back into the past' (Bergson, 1911: 49). Pre-phenomenally, then, there is only flux. Seen from this point of view, the present moment only comes into existence as a discrete entity once it becomes *phenomenal* for us, once we become focused upon and consciously aware of it: an operation we can only perform once the moment is past (Schutz, 1972: 51).

We do not, often, find ourselves in this 'phenomenal' *now*, consciously and self-reflexively meditating on our own duration, on our own situation in the present ('it is now, now'). We are, however, always in the 'phenomenological' *now*, the present moment in which we perpetually and inevitably experience the world, whether we think about it or not.

How does this idea of the phenomenological *now* relate to the notion of the vicinity which I have been pursuing in this section? Simply put, in my vicinity it is always *now*, this phenomenological *now* of my encounter with the world, just as it is always *here*: self-evidently so, if my vicinity is nothing other than a domain whose outer limits are circumscribed by the limits of perceptual space and where I am perpetually and ineluctably at the centre.

What of those situations where two or more vicinities maximally overlap: face-to-face or canonical encounters? In the canonical situation, as we saw in

Chapter 1, space maps onto place. Co-presence, in other words, entails co-spatiality, the congregation of diverse phenomena within one locale with a shared or near-shared set of spatial relations to their environment. We can now refine this description further, to include a notion of *co-temporality*. If it is definitional for a vicinity that it is always *here* and always *now*, then it must be both *here* and *now* in the intersecting vicinities of any co-present others as well as in my own. This phenomenological *now* of myself and of other individuals, furthermore, is the same *now*: we inhabit the same emergent present, the 'instantaneous which dies and is born again endlessly' (Bergson, 1911: 211). This is a basic and fundamental assumption without which my encounters with the world would fall apart in short order. As Schutz puts it (1972: 163): 'The face-to-face situation presupposes ... an actual simultaneity with each other of two separate streams of consciousness'.

This situation changes not one whit, furthermore, when one or more individuals exit the scene. When we leave the site of a face-to-face encounter we carry off with us the phenomenological *now* of our encounter with the world. Our vicinities become discrete, isolated and detached from the vicinities of those we have left, but they nevertheless remain *simultaneous*, unfolding in tandem whether they interconnect with each other or not. This can be amply demonstrated by ringing up to interact with the place where we were ('What are you doing now?'), where only an assumption of co-temporality will warrant the interaction. The same is true, to go back to my earlier examples, of my sister asleep in Canada, my husband snoozing in Plymouth and the party-goers in Polynesia: for all of us, at all times, it is the *now* (the *now* of 4.30 a.m. on Saturday, the *now* of 11.30 p.m. on Friday) of an always-new present moment; an *intersubjective now* held in common by all vicinities everywhere at the moment of their unfolding. The same holds true, too, of Schutz in his garden in the 1940s: everyone everywhere is inhabiting the same present moment in which Schutz is regarding his table, his writing paper, the lake and the mountain; all elsewheres are at once.

It is just precisely this *simultaneity of elsewheres* which permits the complex connectivity which the instantaneity of electronic interaction brings in its wake. By switching on my computer, television or radio, by calling someone on a phone I can instantly avail myself of an interaction with one of an apparent infinity of other localities, each of them transpiring precisely in tandem with my own. For so long as that interaction endures, some aspects of that remote vicinity will overlap with my own, giving me access to the sights and sounds of an elsewhere that may be hundreds or thousands of miles from where I am. This is the activity which would seem to be barred to Schutz: he cannot access the endlessly unfolding elsewheres which exactly accompany his survey of his garden. Only a device capable of instantaneous communication can deliver the simultaneous to us in the moment in which it is unfolding.

2.3   The Electronic Sublime

The account of complex connectivity in the previous section is a typical phenomenologist's manoeuvre, seeking to render the taken-for-granted strange or unfamiliar in order to examine the extraordinary complexity of everyday lived experience. So rapidly have mediated encounters become a fundamental element in our routine engagement with the world – in some cultures at least – that their workings appear unremarkable and their complicated underpinnings in time and space a routinized element of our mundane moment-to-moment encounters with other individuals and with the localities they inhabit. But such was not always the case. A considerable sense of wonder – and in some cases a measure of alarm – frequently accompanied the development of technologies of instantaneous communication. The first message sent over Morse's telegraph link between Washington, DC and Baltimore, Maryland when the commercial telegraph network was inaugurated in 1843 ('What Hath God Wrought!') nicely demonstrates the profound sense of awe that accompanied early real-time encounters-at-a-distance.[5] Such encounters were not without their potential terrors. Peters cites an article of 1920 in the *Atlantic Monthly*, 'written in the voice of a neurasthenic woman' who comments: 'It is bad to hear myself talk on any occasion. It is worse to talk into an empty black hole, without the comfort and guide of a responsive face before me' (Peters, 1999: 198), and Kern, in a similar vein, quotes the 'indefatigable alarmist', the writer Max Nordau, writing in 1892 that it 'would take a century for people to be able "to read a dozen square yards of newspapers daily, to be constantly called to the telephone, to be thinking simultaneously of the five continents of the world" without injury to the nerves' (Kern, 1983: 70). Alongside the stress of the new, however, was the thrill of what Carey (1989: 139) refers to as the 'electronic sublime' with its sometimes feverish imaginings of the shifts in human communicability which new technologies of communication might bring about. The sinking of the *Titanic* in 1912, as Kern argues, served as an early focal point for such sentiments. Through the wonders of wireless telegraphy the first rescue ship was able to be on the scene within two hours, and the news had travelled around the world by the next morning, prompting the following encomium from the *New York Times* eleven days after the event:

> Night and day all year round the millions upon the earth and the thousands upon the sea now reach out and grasp the thin air and use it as a thing more potent for human aid than any strand of wire or cable that was ever spun or woven ... But for the almost magic use of the air the Titanic tragedy would have been shrouded in the secrecy that not so long ago was the power of the sea ... Few New Yorkers realize that all through the roar of the big city there are constantly speeding messages between people separated by vast distances, and that over housetops and even through the walls of buildings and in the very air one breathes are words written by electricity.

(Kern, 1983: 67)[6]

Kern argues persuasively that the development of electronic forms of communication was responsible for a major shift in the way individuals conceptualized

---

[5]See http://www.acmi.net.au/AIC/What_Hath_God_Wrought.html (accessed 15 August 2005).

[6]Telegraphy was also responsible for a considerable degree of confusion on this occasion, as a telegram was sent by the ship's owners some 18 hours after the ship sank, saying that passengers were 'all safe'. I am indebted to Myra Macdonald for pointing this out to me.

the present. By making it possible to 'be in two places at once' (Kern, 1983: 88), electronic communication allowed its participants to experience reality as a multiplicity of disparate events, each of which was unfolding in a present moment which was simultaneous with the *now* of their own private time:

> The present was no longer limited to one event in one place, sandwiched tightly between past and future and limited to local surroundings. In the age of intrusive electronic communication 'now' became an extended interval of time that could, indeed must, include events around the world. Telephone switchboards, telephonic broadcasts, daily newspapers, World Standard Time, and the cinema mediated simultaneity through technology.
>
> (Kern, 1983: 314)

Simultaneity, of course, was not a phenomenon that was brought into existence through the instantaneity or near-instantaneity of electronic communication. Always and at all moments innumerable sequences of events are transpiring in places remote from our own, whether we are aware of them or not. But before the development of devices capable of bringing aspects of the world into the immediate presence of remote individuals, events could not be immediately accessed at a distance. Their contours, the precise directions in which they might develop, could be known only in outline and after-the-event, the time lag being determined on the one hand by the spatial distance between the unfolding situation and the interested individual and on the other by the kinds of space-binding technologies which were available to report on them. With the technologies of instantaneity, on the other hand, events which are occurring simultaneously but elsewhere can be brought into the individual's phenomenological *now* as things to be experienced in the real time of their unfolding. The near-instantaneity of electronic communication – its ability to deliver information across space in the moment in which it is transmitted – permits us to actively experience the world as an apparently endless series of parallel events transpiring precisely in tandem with occurrences in our own immediate vicinity; an awareness which Thompson refers to as 'despatialized simultaneity':

> In earlier historical periods the experience of simultaneity – that is, of events occurring 'at the same time' – presupposed a specific locale in which the simultaneous events could be experienced by the individual. Simultaneity presupposed locality; 'the same time' presupposed 'the same place'. But with the uncoupling of space and time brought about by telecommunication, the experience of simultaneity was detached from the spatial condition of common locality. It became possible to experience events as simultaneous despite the fact that they occurred in locales that were spatially remote. In contrast to the concreteness of the here and now, there emerged a sense of 'now' which was no longer bound to a particular locale. Simultaneity was extended in space and became ultimately global in scope.
>
> (Thompson, 1995: 32)

Instantaneity, furthermore, does not only make tangible the multiple and parallel event-series which are always and everywhere in the process of unfolding in our absence; it also fundamentally changes the conditions under which we relate to and act upon the world. It has been a basic tenet of much writing on human geography over the last several decades that the evolution of new forms of communication and transportation has fundamentally shifted relationships in space and time. In particular, such 'space-adjusting' technologies (Brunn and Leinbach, 1991; Janelle, 1991) are said to shrink distance, so that locales converge in terms of both cost (the expenditure involved in getting to or contacting one location from another) and time.

The motorboat on Schutz's lake will serve as a good example here. The boat, as we have seen, has the potential to bring the absent world into the garden in two related ways. As a form of *transportation* it can physically move objects and people into the here-and-now of immediate perceptual space. The possibility of using some kind of line-of-sight signalling mechanism such as semaphoring, in addition, means that instantaneous *communication* can be effected from the periphery of this perceptual space into the centre, where it can be recognized and read by any individual possessing the appropriate skills to decode the message.

Taken together, transportation and communication thus permit what Harvey (1990: 240) refers to as *space-time compression* and Janelle (1968, 1973) as *time-space convergence*: they 'reduce' distance by shortening the time and the cost of reaching one place from another. The trip from Edinburgh to London, for instance, as Janelle points out, took around four days by stagecoach in 1776, but at Janelle's time of writing took only three hours by plane, including the time taken to travel at each end from city-centre to airport. Seen from this perspective, Edinburgh and London have been 'approaching each other in time-space at the average rate of 29.3 minutes per year for the last 190 years' (Janelle, 1968: 6). A similar calculation has Lansing and Detroit converging by nine minutes a year since 1840 (Janelle, 1973: 9). Harvey, likewise, demonstrates the way in which innovations in transport have served to 'annihilate space through time' (Harvey, 1990: 241) via a diagram illustrating the shrinking globe, with 10 miles per hour travelling time by horse-drawn coaches and sailing ships between 1500 and 1840 increasing to a top speed of 65 miles per hour by steam trains by 1930, and considerably higher speeds by propeller aircraft in the 1950s and jet planes in 1990. The globe in Harvey's accompanying graphic, meanwhile, gets smaller and smaller.

Just as each of these developments in transportation serves to effectively compress distance through increased velocity, so modern communications technologies similarly work to converge places the one with the other. Space thus becomes thoroughly relativized, operating as a function of the time it takes to traverse it electronically: absolute location – individuals' distance from each other in physical space – becomes less significant in a range of interactive circumstances than does relative location, the degree of connectivity between remote sites (Brunn and Leinbach, 1991: xviii). As Gould writes:

> [M]any spaces … are not strictly metric at all, because we cannot measure distances between places symmetrically and as people actually experience them. In fact, for many spaces of great geographic importance the very notion of metricity may not be pertinent. What may be much more important is the simple fact of how people and things are

connected together. It is the sheer connectivity of things that creates many spaces of interest.

(Gould, 1991: 10)

Consider our forced exile some streets away from Schutz's garden, which was the outcome of our uninvited attempts to directly penetrate the immediate perceptual space of the other. Measured by degrees of connectivity, we are a considerable distance away from our target, stuck with such limited and time-delaying options as finding a telegraph office or postbox and waiting for our communication to be physically carried to the appropriate place, or – the best option – finding a telephone box, calling his house and waiting for whoever answers the phone to call him in to the house. Teleport a mobile phone into Schutz's immediate vicinity, though, and we can contact him in a fraction of a second, significantly compressing the time it will take to reach one place from another. The mobile phone will effectively 'shrink space' for us, bringing us almost immediately into the presence of the absent other.

One repercussion of this shrinking of space is the simultaneous expansion of what Janelle calls *human extensibility* (Janelle, 1973, 1991). Extensibility, as Janelle points out, is the corollary of time-space convergence: as places move closer together in travel or communication time, so individuals and places extend their interactive range over larger and larger areas of absolute space. This is, of course, not only true of electronic forms of communication: Schutz's two books, as we have seen, allow remote discourses to penetrate the local space of his immediate vicinity, and if a newspaper or magazine were to turn out to be one of the 'other things' on his writing table then the same would hold true, insofar as all varieties of mediated communication permit us to act and be acted upon at a distance, at least in the limited sense of conveying or receiving information that can potentially influence some aspect of our behaviour or view of the world. The media of instantaneous communication, however, allow us to extend ourselves in space in the *now* of our own personal time, so that our utterances have the potential to be heard at the moment we produce them. Nor, in an era of globalization, is human extensibility limited to the exchange of verbal messages pure and simple. Global markets, cyber-activism, remote weapons systems, the satellite technology that permits live television to enter into and shape the contours of events at remote locations are all examples of the concrete penetration of electronic forms of communication into the fabric of everyday existence at a distance.

2.4   The Phenomenology of Electronic Communication

Janelle's discussion of human extensibility may at first glance appear to have a great deal in common with McLuhan's view of global communications as the extension of 'our central nervous system itself in a global embrace, abolishing both space and time as far as our planet is concerned' (McLuhan, 1973: 11). We should, however, treat this formula with some caution. *Time-space distanciation* – the dislocation of social relations from the 'particularities of contexts of presence' (Giddens, 1990: 20) – may indeed allow us to be positioned by events and discourses at a distance in the *now* of their unfolding. As Moores (1995: 331) argues,

> at the heart of time-space distanciation processes lies a complex reordering of the conditions of presence and absence. Not only are our interactions with others not confined to a bounded locale, but our lives are also touched to a greater extent by forces and happenings from far away. Places become 'phantasmagoric': 'thoroughly penetrated by and shaped in terms of social influences quite distant from them'.

(Giddens, 1990: 19)

To argue that lives are 'touched ... by forces and happenings from far away', though, is to argue neither that space and time are abolished nor that instantaneous communication somehow serves to actually relocate us to a remote place, to be other than where we are. When I encounter a remote place through the mediation of electronic communication, aspects of that locale will become temporarily part of my vicinity, available to be seen and heard at a distance. But encounters with a mediated world are, as we have seen, limited by comparison with face-to-face encounters in terms of the breadth of sensory experience that is available to an individual: television, for instance, as Meyrowitz (1986: 258) puts it, 'conveys a limited amount of sensory information, and thus abstracts for the viewer only a fraction of the contingencies of actual physical presence', and the same remains true of other varieties of encounter-at-a-distance. For time and space to be abolished, even in the limited metaphorical sense that we might come to have a strong sense of 'being there' in a remote environment, we would need to believe ourselves to be relocated to some other locale. It seems clear, however, that our all-encompassing situatedness in the place where we are rules out any notion of our actually, physically feeling ourselves to be elsewhere, particularly if that elsewhere can present itself to us only through the limited modalities of sight and sound and can therefore offer us only a relatively thin rendition of the remote place. When 'the instantaneous interface replaces the face-to-face' (Virilio, 1991: 326), we are unlikely to mistake the one for the other.

Space-binding technologies, then, do not abolish time and space; nor do they cause them to wither away. How, then, are we to understand the discussion in this chapter of vicinities and of the momentary overlapping of vicinities afforded by instantaneous or near-instantaneous media of communication? Put simply, the changes brought about by the development of the electronic media are *phenomenological*: it is our *experience* of the world, at both an interpersonal and global level which is transformed by electronic communication. At an interpersonal level, as we have seen, encounters with distant others bring elements of the remote world momentarily within the bounds of an individual's perceptual field, to be experienced – albeit somewhat thinly – for so long as the interaction continues. At a global level, as Kern has argued, it has become commonplace, in western cultures at least, to conceive of the world as an apparently endless series of simultaneous elsewheres whose unfolding events may impinge upon and affect to a greater or lesser degree what is transpiring in our own locales. We should, though, remain wary both of McLuhan's notion of the abolition of space and time, and of Kern's own suggestion that such historical shifts in conceptualizations of time and space permit us to be 'in two places at once'.

One further note of caution needs to be sounded. Electronic telecommunication devices, as I have demonstrated in this chapter, permit their users to interact with a simultaneous elsewhere: a distant place in which events are transpiring in tandem with events in an individual's own vicinity. When I switch on the radio or the television, or ring up a friend, my interaction with those devices is predicated upon my belief that it is *now* in that distant place of enunciation just as it is *now* in my own. All have in common that they are capable of transmitting instantly or near instantly from a source to a receiver. Instantaneity, then, is not simply an *affordance* of electronic media; it would also appear to be *ontological*, part of the essential nature of such devices.

Furthermore, instantaneity is, as we have seen, predicated on simultaneity. Electronic communication can only deliver information instantly or near-instantly because everywhere is unfolding at once. The gallery of the news studio where an editor is selecting which feed should appear on my television screen, the street nearby where my friend is talking to me on her mobile phone, the room in another city where my sister is about to press the send button on an instant messenger screen on her computer, the room in my house where I may be watching the news or talking to my friend on the phone or waiting to type my reply into the messenger screen, are all situated in the same present moment.

Does electronically mediated communication, then, always bring us the world in the moment of its unfolding? Not necessarily. An important distinction needs be drawn between the instantaneity of electronic communication – its ability to send information instantly so that it arrives in the same moment (more or less) as it was transmitted – and its potential for *immediacy*, for delivering an elsewhere which is unfolding in the intersubjective *now* of my encounter with the world. Instantaneity, as I have said, would appear to be a necessary property of electronic forms of communication, but immediacy is contingent upon the temporal status of the material transmitted. When I listen to the radio, I may hear someone who is speaking to me right now, or music that is being played live in a concert hall somewhere. I am as likely, however, to be listening to a voice or a piece of music that was recorded earlier. When I use my computer for video-conferencing or to download streaming media I will see and hear someone performing gestures and uttering remarks at the moment of my attending to them, or at least as near to the moment as my computer can deliver them; but when I read the latest communications on an electronic message board, although the messages flash up near-instantaneously on my screen they will have been written some minutes, hours or days earlier. In each case the events and/or the information that enters into my vicinity through the mediation of these devices will be instantaneously or near-instantaneously transmitted to me because of the simultaneity of source (a radio transmitter; a server) and receiver; but only in some of them (the live broadcast; the streaming video) does that instantaneous transmission offer me an immediate encounter with an elsewhere which is unfolding in my own present moment.

Most electronic media, then, do not always and under all circumstances deliver immediacy: although they allow us to receive messages and encounter events in the moment in which they are *transmitted*, they do not always permit us to receive messages in the moment in which they are *produced*, or to encounter events in the moment in which they transpire. Telephones would seem to be an exception here: to have a phone conversation is to engage in an interaction which is not only instantaneous – received in the same moment as it is sent – but also immediate, connecting me with an individual who is listening even as I am speaking. Answerphones apart, telephone conversations of necessity involve this coincidence of message production and reception. Most electronic devices, however, afford both immediate encounters and also time-delayed forms of communication, where it is a message produced earlier or an event in the past which is instantly transmitted from source to receiver. The slice of the world which I interact with at-a-distance through the mediation of electronic communication, in other words, may or may not be unfolding in the *now* of my encounter with it. This will turn out to be an important distinction as we turn, at last, to a consideration of the phenomenology of live television.

Part II
The Live Event

3

The Meaning of Live

3.1 Introduction

It is just after 9.16 p.m. on 14 April 1958. Live from the BBC's *Panorama* studio, British presenter Richard Dimbleby exhorts the audience at home to note the time on the wall clock behind him. This 'has all to do', he says, with a machine called Vera, or Vision Electronic Recording Apparatus. The programme cuts to the BBC's Research Department in South London, where scientists can be seen prowling around a machine. Dimbleby asks one of them to turn off the machine, and the programme then cuts back to Dimbleby, who asks the viewer to note the time on the clock again, now standing at 9.20 p.m. 'When this clock jumps back suddenly', announces Dimbleby, 'you're on the telerecording by Vera'. Dimbleby's image is replaced by a fuzzy shot of the clock, showing 9.16, followed by a repeat of his early introduction. Finally, there is a cut to Dimbleby in the studio, coughing humorously. 'Well, there you are', he says. 'That's where we came in, in a way. That was the beginning of Panorama tonight just about five minutes after I first did it. This is now me again really'.

Dimbleby had just demonstrated for the first time on British television the British answer to the new Ampex video recording equipment, developed in the United States in 1956. Later in 1958, the BBC would itself start to use Ampex at its Lime Grove studios. Up until that point, British television had depended to a considerable extent on live broadcasting, with the exception of feature film presentations, short filmed inserts for live drama, and poor-quality telerecordings produced by kinescopes, machines that filmed live material directly from television monitors for subsequent re-broadcast. With the air of a conjuror displaying an extraordinary trick for the first time, Dimbleby now offered his audience the novelty of communication delayed, of the moment frozen on tape for near-instant re-encounter and perusal. If, in the early years of the twentieth century, the instantaneity of electronic communication was a source of alarm and wonderment, then for that moment in 1958 it was the non-live, the replayable, which was the marvel.

In the US, where television was largely dependent on telefilm, more than 70% of prime-time transmissions were already non-live by 1957 (Vianello, 1985: 33). With the development of videotape technology would come the additional benefits of shooting broadcast material in real time – 'as live', with full continuity (Bourdon, 2000: 539) – but transmitting it later. Liveness would increasingly come to be a genre- and niche-dependent phenomenon, associated, mostly, with ceremonial occasions, sporting matches, catastrophes, one-off spectaculars, shopping channels and certain kinds of reality television broadcast. Live television would remain capable of attracting large viewing figures: in the US, some 166 million viewers would tune in to the live network coverage in the aftermath of the Kennedy assassination in 1963;[1] and more recently, in Britain, some 31 million would watch the funeral of Princess Diana in 1997,[2] whilst the live news reports of the attack on the World Trade Center on 11 September 2001 would attract a domestic audience of over 16 million viewers, a 70% audience share.[3] Despite these impressive demographics, however, by the end of the twentieth century most television transmissions on most channels were no longer live.

Increasingly, too, programmes advertised to the audience as live would consist of a patchwork of properly 'live' material – material 'transmitted and received in the same moment as it is produced' (Ellis, 1992: 132) – and inserts filmed or taped earlier. A quick overview of a morning's viewing on American television on one particular extraordinary day will make clear the extent to which even broadcasts overtly promoted as 'live' can, in fact, only intermittently claim that status.

3.2   The Look of Live: The Live Breakfast Show

At 8 a.m. Eastern Time on 11 September 2001, the American networks and cable news channels were airing live breakfast shows: *NBC News Today* (NBC), *The Early Show* (CBS), *Good Morning America* (ABC), *Imus on MSNBC* (MSNBC), *Fox and Friends* (Fox News Channel) and *CNN Live at Daybreak* (CNN). With the exception of *Imus on MSNBC*, which featured the shock jock Don Imus and his associates speaking into radio microphones, the grammar of these programmes was remarkably similar. Each programme was fronted by two or three presenters, either at a newsdesk or in a more casual chat-show setting, bantering with each other and trailing or introducing upcoming segments. Each programme, too, featured the same kinds of segments: news, weather, traffic, feature stories and interviews, either in the studio (NBC, CBS, ABC, Fox News) or down-the-line with a guest at a remote location (MSNBC, CNN).

To a viewer randomly channel-hopping on this particular morning, the 'liveness' of these programmes should have been relatively self-evident. CNN's programme styled itself as live in its title, *CNN Live at Daybreak*. Several of the programmes also announced their liveness through chromakeyed legends on the screen: *CNN Live* (CNN), *MSNBC Live* (MSNBC), *GMA Live EDT* (ABC), *Live White House/Live Los Angeles* (CBS). In addition, presenters occasionally made reference to the live status of particular upcoming segments:

> And this is live, by the way, it's really gonna happen at 9 o'clock. (Presenter, ABC, trailing a live remote)

---

[1] Schramm, 1965: 14.
[2] http://news.bbc.co.uk/1/hi/entertainment/tv_and_radio/1921737.stm (accessed 1 February 2005).
[3] http://ads.guardian.co.uk/html.ng/Params.richmedia=yes&location=middle&site=Guardian&section=108926&country=gbr&rand=1091522530281749&spacedesc=50 (accessed 15 March 2005).

Other programme elements similarly worked to steer viewers towards the conclusion that what they were watching was live. Vianello (1985) suggests that there are two key elements which act as indices of liveness: direct address – a gaze to camera, accompanied by a discourse that seemingly directly targets the audience at home – and remoteness. Both of these elements were present in abundance. Anchors, newsreaders, weather reporters and correspondents all intermittently addressed their remarks directly to camera; and all of the programmes featured material from remote locations, although in MSNBC's case this took the form of real-time telephone interviews from the Imus studio. A certain absence of glossiness, characteristic of particular species of live daytime magazine programmes (Moores, 1995) was also in evidence: spill cries (Goffman, 1981: 102; Moores, 1995: 339) which perform a kind of backstage behaviour (Goffman, 1978) indicative of spontaneity; ostensibly ad-lib outbreaks of joking and teasing between (particularly) male and female anchors; open references to real-time processes in the studio, such as the need to allow time for the NBC camera to get to the newsdesk for the 8 a.m. news bulletin.

Taken singly, of course, each of these elements can also be found in non-live contexts. Direct address to camera turns up in ad breaks and in other kinds of edited footage as well. Cuts to elsewhere do not necessarily require that both sites are simultaneous. Spill cries and pratfalls, indicative of the less-than-perfect control which characterizes events that are unfolding in real time, can readily be performed to supply the *look* of the live in material that is actually pre-recorded and/or edited. Taken jointly, however, in the larger context of the overall aesthetic or stylization (Caldwell, 1995) overlaying the programmes, each of these elements played a role in marking the material as live. Thus while direct address by itself will not act as a guarantor of liveness, it will do so when accompanied by an on-screen clock showing the current time and date, which strongly warrants the inference that the presenter is addressing the audience even as they watch. Cuts to remote locations are similarly warranted as live when the handovers between studio and remotes are accompanied by real-time badinage between personnel in the different locations, which foregrounds and renders transparent the simultaneity of the two sites. Ineptitude, performed or otherwise, may well be enough to convince viewers that what they are watching is happening *now*:

> Is it live? The answer might come from textual indices: a host looks us straight in the eyes, in the flat lighting of the video, and starts stammering, then apologises. We tend to think, routinely, that we are seeing a live programme.
>
> (Bourdon, 2000: 539)

Taken together, then, all of these elements would have served to offer the surfing viewer a surfeit of information concerning the liveness of the material on screen. Displays, disingenuous or otherwise, of backstage behaviour; gaze to camera and direct interpellation of the audience at home; interactive exchanges in real time with remote locations; calendrical information which identified segments as unfolding in the *now* of the viewer's encounter with them; explicit graphic and verbal references to liveness: for the teleliterate viewer, likely already primed with a set of generic expectations about morning magazine shows, it might well have seemed like a breach of the contract between audience and broadcaster if the programme in its entirety was to have turned out to have been recorded. Not that this would have been technically impossible: two-ways between the studio and remotes necessarily involve simultaneity between the two locations, but could have been recorded earlier, in a time frame that was not concurrent with the viewer's watching of them; the on-screen clock could have indexed the time of transmission but not the time of events unfolding in the studio; bungling and fumbling could be indicative of 'continuity' material (Bourdon, 2000: 538), material shot 'as live' in one continuous take but not transmitted as it is shot; and the 'live' graphic, when it manifested itself on the screen, could have been being used to indicate simply that events were occurring in real time (a 'live performance') without lip-synching or other such markers of miming. Conventionally, though, at least in daytime magazine shows and other kinds of programmes that promote themselves as live, to mark material graphically as 'live' if only this latter kind of meaning is intended might well be to risk an accusation of bad faith.

It would seem fair to say, in summary, that the breakfast shows on American television on this particular morning were clearly performing themselves as live, as offering to the viewer an encounter with an immediate elsewhere. A closer examination of the broadcasts, however, will readily demonstrate that by no means all of the material on offer was live, at least in the 'full' or 'maximum' sense (Bourdon, 2000: 534) that the time of the television event and the time of transmission and the time of reception are one and the same (Heath and Skirrow, 1977: 53). Certainly, some segments of the programmes satisfied this criterion: the newsreader's address to the studio camera, the weather reporter's vox pops on the street, the larking-about of the presenters, the real-time chats with guests in the studios. But other, pre-recorded elements were equally present, embedded within and subordinate to this overarching live framing (Tolson, 1996: 63). The programmes cut away from the newsreader delivering her lines (to the camera, in the moment in which they were received by the audience at home) to news footage recorded and edited earlier. The direct address, 'fully' live, of a presenter in the studio book-ended a recorded feature story. At regular intervals, the live studio flow was supplanted by advertising segments and channel idents in the form of edited montages of images and sound.

On the whole, the broadcasters demonstrated considerable care in the way they signalled these alternations between the fully live, the as-live and the recorded. Give or take a few moments here or there as the programmes caught up with themselves during the real time of transmission, the chromakeyed legend 'live' would appear or disappear from the screen as the broadcasts shifted from moment to moment from live to non-live material and back again. One 15-minute stretch of *CNN Live at Daybreak*, for instance, consisted of the following segments:

08.34   Live, studio
08.34   Graphic, 'Eye of the storm'
08.34   Live link to Florida, two-way chat

08.34	Florida live, hurricane piece to camera
08.34	Florida, recorded footage
08.38	Florida live, hurricane piece to camera
08.38	Graphic, *CNN presents* ...
08.38	Live, studio
08.38	Live link to weather report
08.38	Live weather report
08.39	Live, studio
08.39	Live link to fashion show
08.39	Ad break
08.42	Live, studio
08.42	Live link to fashion show, two-way chat
08.42	Live fashion show
08.45	Sponsor statement/ad break
08.47	Live 'Money Matters', piece to camera
08.48	'Money Matters' recorded footage + live voiceover
08.48	Live 'Money Matters', piece to camera

The use of the *CNN Live* graphic mapped fairly flawlessly on to the alternations between live and recorded material in this instance, as a closer examination of the 'hurricane' story in Florida, and the 'Money Matters' segment will reveal. Both segments started and finished with a live address, live in the 'full' sense that the presenter was uttering the words to camera in the same moment as they were transmitted by the broadcaster and received on any television tuned into the channel. Both also incorporated edited and pre-recorded material. The hurricane story featured an edited sequence of images of the Florida coastline. This edited material did not carry the 'live' graphic, despite a clear attempt to preserve 'as-live' continuity by featuring the same presenter speaking to camera and wearing the same outfit and adopting a similar stance as in his live performance. 'Money Matters' cut to an edited montage of material during the presenter's live address; the word 'live' disappeared from the screen each time one of these montages appeared, despite the continued live voiceover from the correspondent. If what was to be seen was not happening *now*, in other words, in the moment of the viewer's apprehension of it, then the channel would not formally mark the material as live. If live television is a 'collage of film, video and "live"', all interwoven into a complex and altered time scheme' (Feuer, 1983: 15), then television, in this instance at least, acted meticulously to alert its audience to the exact temporal status of what was on offer; and what was on offer was just precisely the continuous ebb and flow of the live and the recorded, the *now* and the *then*, the raw and the cooked.

3.3   Going Live: 9/11

The live magazine shows on this particular morning seem, in retrospect, pretty much routine. Any viewer tuning in on an average morning that year would have encountered an essentially similar blend of live-to-camera pieces and live two-ways, as-live continuity material, edited montages of sound and image, ad breaks, pre-recorded station idents and the like. Nothing out of the ordinary was going on, apparently, either in the studios or in the simultaneous elsewheres into which the studios occasionally dipped as one segment segued into another in the live space of the broadcast. As one CBS presenter would comment, shortly after 8.30 a.m., 'It's kinda quiet around the country. We like quiet'.

The routinized and taken-for-granted nature of these broadcasts might lead us to question whether they provide the best possible case study for monitoring the 'liveness' of the live. Such programmes tend to have running orders established and set in motion well before they air. It might therefore seem predictable that they would contain considerable quantities of non-live material, given their reasonably elaborate 'forestructuring' (Scannell, 1999: 29) by the broadcasters.

Such an argument would suggest that we need to consider other kinds of live broadcast to see whether there yet remain corners and niches in the broadcast schedule where uninterrupted liveness – a continuous flow of material unfolding on the television screen in the same instant as it transpires elsewhere – is to be found. Fast-forwarding a mere 15 minutes from the CBS comment ('it's too quiet' was its prescient conclusion) will take us into precisely the kind of situation where we might most expect to encounter such a phenomenon.

Somewhere between 8.48 and 8.53 a.m. Eastern Time, as breaking news of an incident involving a plane and one of the towers of the World Trade Center reached the broadcasters, each of the channels was to abandon its scheduled programming. CNN broke abruptly into a statement from its sponsor at 8.48 a.m. with a live shot of the building accompanied by a voiceover from its anchor. Fox News came back from an ad break at 8.50 a.m. to a three-shot of its presenters in the studio and a strap bearing the words: 'Fox News Alert: Plane Crashes into World Trade Center'. ABC cut at 8.51 a.m. from a promo for its evening programme *ABC Nightline* to a two-shot of its studio presenters breaking the news; and on MSNBC, the channel cut unceremoniously from Don Imus in mid-sentence to its *Breaking News* ident, followed by a two-shot of its newsdesk anchors. Only on NBC, where the presenter was initially unable to show the live shot when he broke the story at 8.51 a.m., was there a small degree of variation. NBC went to an ad break, before coming back to its live catastrophe coverage shortly afterwards.

By 8.53 a.m., five minutes after the first plane hit the North Tower, all the channels were showing near-identical images of the World Trade Center, to the accompaniment of live voiceover commentaries.

In such a situation, we would clearly expect a dramatic shift in the ratio of fully live to recorded material. And indeed, until a little after 9.02 a.m. – for some nine to twelve minutes, depending on the time at which each broadcaster turned its schedules over to catastrophe coverage – the material was fully live. During the core nine minutes between 8.53 and 9.02, a surfing viewer would have encountered something remarkably similar on each channel: raw footage of the burning building, accompanied by the real-time voices of anchors in the studio and eyewitnesses on the telephone calling from locations in New York where they could see or had seen the impact of the plane.

As there would be no ad breaks, no sponsor statements and no trailers or channel idents thereafter for some hours or days on each channel, it might seem reasonable to assume that what would follow, minute on minute and hour on hour, would be that rarest and most elusive of televisual forms, the fully live broadcast. Even here, however, this would turn out not to be the case. Mellencamp has written in a related context about the compulsion of live catastrophe coverage to replay raw footage in an attempt at 'mastery and discharge' (Mellencamp, 1990: 246), and the live coverage of 9/11 would be no exception. The live television event played the same brief loops over and over again, insistently cutting into the live flow of the broadcast to re-display the mesmerizing instant of impact. From a visual point of view the opening moments of the event were, as is frequently the case with disasters and catastrophes, lost to history; but the impact of the second plane on the South Tower at 9.02 a.m. was broadcast live, and the compulsion to rewind and review the material was plain, not least because several of the anchors were in mid-sentence at that moment, and/or did not have a clear enough view on their studio monitors to make sense of what they were seeing. Requests to re-rack the tape so that the footage could be viewed again swiftly followed, and the pattern which would dominate the next several hours of broadcasting was set. Anchors on ABC, for instance, would ask to look at the image again at 9.03 a.m., less than a minute after the impact itself; and again at 9.05 a.m.; and again at 9.07, 9.10 and so on. On some channels the tape would, in addition, be looped to show the same impact, sometimes from different camera perspectives, again and again as part of the same short segment. As the hours went by, these frequent repetitions would be augmented in turn by other kinds of recorded footage: replays of other significant moments, such as the collapse in turn of each of the two towers; statements from politicians; wildly panning raw footage of individuals running away from the explosions; vox pops from people on the street. So dense in the end was the interweaving of the immediate past with the present on the television screen, and so rapid was the escalation of unforeseeable events, that the anchors occasionally found themselves adrift in a sea of temporal chaos, unsure whether what they were looking at was a novel occurrence or a replay of something that had already happened:

We're we're going to cut away from the live pictures for just a moment to replay uh what just happened and I thought when when it first happened I thought it was a replay but in fact we saw this live perhaps two minutes ago look at that a jet plane clearly a jet plane a good sized airplane slamming into the second tower of the WTC.

(Anchor, Fox News, 9.03 a.m.)

Or as one dazed anchor on ABC would put it, gazing at re-racked footage of the North Tower, some minutes after it had collapsed: 'Here's a picture that doesn't exist any more'.

3.4   The Ontology of Liveness

> Thanks for watching the show this week, you can watch it again tonight if you missed
> it earlier on, but if you missed it earlier on you won't be able to hear me saying this,
> so what the heck am I talking about?
>
>   (Chris Evans, *TFI Friday*, 28 March 1997)

As my brief examination of live television on 11 September 2001 suggests, even
those varieties of television which we might be most likely to think of as 'fully'
or 'maximally' live are unlikely to be any such thing. Daytime magazine shows,
as we have seen, will segue apparently effortlessly between recorded features,
collages of actuality footage taped earlier and fully live studio segments. The
same is true, *mutatis mutandis*, of other varieties of live broadcasting. Classic
ceremonial events will draw upon library footage to amplify and contextualize
the images that are unfolding in the real time of the broadcast: sequences of shots
panning across old battlefields, war cemeteries and poppy fields, for instance, in
the case of an event such as the annual Remembrance Day ceremony in London,
or a montage of soft-focus shots of Princess Diana with her children on the
occasion of her funeral. Such moments will generally be supplemented, too, by
re-racked images of earlier elements of the event as it continues to develop,
often increasing in length and frequency as the main stages of the event appear
to be drawing to a close. Live catastrophe coverage, in its early stages, may
appear to be the least dependent on library footage and pre-recorded segments,
for the simple reason that television has, to an extent, been caught unawares.
Rapidly, however, replays of striking or spectacular elements of the event will
begin to make their appearance on the screen, and once again, as time passes
archive footage and talking-head replays will begin to cut increasingly into the
live space of the broadcast. Even channels apparently (momentarily or otherwise)
dedicated to live transmissions will very likely turn out to be dependent to
one extent or another on some variety of time-delay mechanism. The British
channel E4, for example, has intermittently handed over substantial amounts
of its daytime schedule to ostensibly live coverage of the goings-on in the
house where the reality programme *Big Brother* is being filmed; such footage
is, however, transmitted with a short time delay so that controversial and/or
potentially actionable material can be removed. The British satellite channel
L!VE TV, needless to say, cuts away from the live flow of the broadcast at
regular intervals for ad breaks and trailers, and also features entire programmes
that consist of pre-recorded talking-head slots and/or continuity footage, held
together by an as-live address to the camera at the beginning and end. It would
appear that the one remaining domain of the fully live is the television shopping
channel, where the need to update potential customers on remaining stocks and
changing prices means that the moment of merchandizing must be simultaneous
with the moment of acquisition. Even here, however, channels can be seen
to cut occasionally to a montage of pre-recorded images of the commodity
on offer, albeit accompanied by a live voiceover from the presenter in the
studio.

Considered from the point of view of the relationship between the event and its transmission, then, television can rarely be said to be fully live in anything other than a fragmentary way. Once questions of reception enter the picture, furthermore, moments of maximal liveness – where the event is viewed even as it transpires – become even rarer. If the machinery of time delay has pervasively insinuated itself into the live flow of the broadcast, then it has done so to even greater effect as far as reception is concerned. Video and DVD equipment permit viewers to record material for subsequent perusal, thereby providing the audience with its own mechanisms of temporal rupture even where none existed in the original broadcast; and more recent developments such as the digital video recorder TiVo (slogan: 'Play with Live TV') or Sky+ in the UK permit viewers to freeze, slow down, rewind, fast-forward and replay live television before, if they wish, re-inserting themselves painlessly into the live flow of the broadcast.

Seen from this perspective, fully live television increasingly begins to look like an endangered species; all the more odd, then, on the face of it, that the ideology of liveness, the idea that television is ontologically, *essentially* live should have remained so remarkably persistent. As Heath and Skirrow were to argue, some twenty years after the introduction of videotape:

> Television covers at least the transmission of cinema films, the transmission of video tape-recorded material, the transmission of film shot for television … and transmission 'live', 'as it happens', unrecorded, *en direct* (the French expression). The last is very far indeed from representing the bulk of the television seen but is nevertheless taken automatically as the television norm, as the very definition of television.

> (Heath and Skirrow, 1977: 53)

On what grounds might liveness be considered to be 'the very definition of television', given that so much of its output involves a disjuncture between the time of production and the time of reception? In considering this question we need to distinguish between television as an apparatus – an electronic device for the reception and display of sound and moving images – and television as a medium; and we will need to draw, too, on the distinction outlined in the previous chapter between instantaneity and immediacy. Instantaneity – simultaneity or near-simultaneity of *transmission* and reception – is, as I argued in Chapter 2, an affordance of all forms of electronic communication, inasmuch as the speed associated with electronic media entails that the message will arrive in the instant or near-instant in which it is sent, unless a further mediating device such as a recorder or a computer server is interposed between message source and receiver. Immediacy – simultaneity or near-simultaneity of an *event* and its reception elsewhere – is also an affordance, but may or may not be realized on a particular occasion, depending on whether the event is transmitted as it transpires, or is captured by means of some species of recording device for transmission later.

It is immediacy, clearly, which is at stake as far as 'fully' live television is concerned. Those segments of *CNN Live at Daybreak* on 11 September 2001 which carried the chromakeyed legend *CNN Live* – the studio chats and links, the weather report, the live 'Money Matters' piece and so on – were unfolding at the same moment (give or take any fractional satellite delay) as the audience were watching them; and when the second plane slammed into the second tower of the World Trade Center, and when one and then the other building collapsed into the street, these events were transpiring in just that moment in which they were being viewed in a multiplicity of simultaneous places. Richard Dimbleby's words to camera – 'This is now me again really' – could similarly be heard as they were uttered by any viewers watching BBC television in Britain at 9.20 p.m. on 14 April 1958. If Dimbleby's elegant little conjuring trick with Vera or the events of 9/11 were to be on television today, however, then I could watch them in the same moment as they are *transmitted*; what I could not do is to watch them as they *happen*. In such a situation the instantaneity of electronic communication would be preserved, but I would not be able to participate in an immediate encounter with a distant elsewhere.

What has this to do with the question of the essential liveness of television? Put simply, some of the arguments in the literature have to do not with immediacy but with either the instantaneous character of the communication or the nature of the apparatus. As an example of the latter, we can consider the view espoused by certain theorists of television aesthetics in the past. For such writers, the key approach to television lay in comparing it with film. Considering the status of the image in each case, attention was drawn to what might have seemed to be a crucial distinction: that while film was both shot and projected one frame at a time, giving it what appeared to be a static quality, television involved the relay of an image that was constantly being made and re-made at the moment of display. To quote Zettl,

> film motion consists actually of nothing but a great number of frozen 'at-at' positions which are shown to the viewer in rapid succession. But nothing moves. We could create the impression of motion quite readily by firing in a predetermined order twenty-four slide projectors per second. While in film each frame is actually a static image, the television image is continually moving, very much in the manner of the Bergsonian durée. The scanning beam is constantly trying to complete an always incomplete image. Even if the image on the screen seems at rest, it is structurally in motion. Each television frame is always in a state of becoming.

(Zettl, 1978: 5)

On this view, television might be said to be perpetually live, simply on the grounds that the image is constantly coming into being; it is, as Heath and Skirrow put it,

> an image in perpetual motion, the movement of a continually scanning beam; whatever the status of the material transmitted, the image as series of electronic impulses is necessarily 'as it happens'.

(Heath and Skirrow, 1977: 53)

Television could thus be viewed as essentially, ontologically live, on the grounds that the image is electronically generated and therefore dynamically renews itself in a perpetual present moment. Does this, however, help to explain why I believe myself to be viewing a live event when watching some kinds of television but not others? It would appear not. The argument from the electronic immediacy of the apparatus provides, certainly, a level of support for anyone wishing to argue that television as a medium is ontologically live, but it does not help to determine why viewers would have believed themselves to be in the grip of a live event when they watched the events of 11 September 2001. On the basis of this analysis, *all* material viewed on television is live. The events of 9/11 and the before-and-after shots of Dimbleby's Vera experiment would clearly be 'live' but so would my subsequent viewings of them, should they turn up at a later date on television in the form of recordings. Indeed, even were I to watch these events on a VCR they would still feature as 'live' on this account; an electronic beam would still be painting the screen, even though the message source was a video in a machine in my room rather than a transmission from elsewhere. If there is an unimpeachable argument to be had about the ontological liveness of television, it is not this.

What other arguments are on offer? The next one proceeds in a somewhat similar vein, but takes as its starting point the instantaneity of television as a medium rather than its mode of operation as an apparatus. Once again a comparison with cinema serves as the point of departure. Cinema presents its product in discrete and bounded slices with a defined beginning and end, so the argument goes, but television constitutes itself – particularly in an era of 24-hour broadcasting – as an apparently endless flow, always available and never pausing. We switch it on and there it is, coming to us from elsewhere in the moment in which we encounter it. Television is thus 'on tap', perpetually domestically accessible on demand like water or gas or electricity. To quote Houston:

> The flow of American television goes on for twenty-four hours a day, which is critical in producing the idea that the text issues from an endless supply that is sourceless, natural, inexhaustible, and co-extensive with psychological reality itself.
>
> (Houston, 1984: 184)

On this account, television would appear to be doubly live: endlessly bringing the absent world to the viewer in the form of an endlessly reconstituted image. Television is always there, always being sent to us *right now*. To switch on the television is to open up an immediate channel of communication, quiescent until the moment that we choose to attend to it but imprinting itself instantaneously on our screens thereafter in an apparently never-endingly transmitted flow. Viewed from this perspective, television can once again be regarded as necessarily live, at least in the sense that the channel of communication operates in real time, offering viewers the perpetual possibility of an interaction with a message which is being transmitted at the moment in which they receive it.

This argument, needless to say, presents similar problems. If I switch on my television now – in my study, at 8.13 a.m. Greenwich Mean Time on a Sunday morning – and channel-surf with my remote, I will be met by a dazzling variety of events, tumbling into my immediate vicinity one by one as I switch from one channel to the next. On some channels, as I encounter them, the images of the world that will momentarily enter my vicinity emanate from a simultaneous elsewhere: a man on a sofa, directly addressing me from a studio in London at 8.13 a.m. GMT; another man behind a desk, directly addressing me from a studio in Atlanta at 3.13 a.m. Eastern Daylight Time; a woman at a desk in Dubai at 11.13 a.m. local time. In each of these places the individuals are speaking at or close to the moment in which I hear and see them. On other channels, the events which are available for me to view happened at another time: some 15 seconds ago, if I am watching *Big Brother Live*; earlier this morning, if I am watching a recorded news story on a rolling news channel; days, weeks, months or years earlier if the channel is showing a documentary or a drama or a film, or some years, decades or centuries in the future if I am viewing the SciFi Channel. In each case I will find myself dipping in and out of the endless flow of material that offers itself to my attention simply by virtue of having switched on my television; but it is only in the first set of instances – the studio-bound individuals reading the news – that I will be afforded an immediate encounter. The instantaneity and constant availability of television, in other words, does not help to explain why liveness – 'transmission "live"', "as it happens"', unrecorded, *en direct*', as Heath and Skirrow put it – might be regarded as part of the essential structure of television: not all of the information which is perpetually available to rush into my vicinity at the touch of my fingers is live.

Only an argument from immediacy, then, will permit us to offer an account of the essential liveness of television. This account would appear, at first glance, to be difficult to sustain, given that the majority of the encounters with the world which are afforded to me by television are not immediate.

One way out of this impasse might be to think of liveness as a set of communicative mechanisms: as an effect, rather than a concrete question of time and space. Television, after all, frequently *performs* immediacy in ways which are not ontologically given but which have devolved, rather, from the communicative imperatives of the medium. Consider, for example, the use in news broadcasts and other related genres of the autocue or teleprompter, which permits anchors to offer their gaze to camera – and thus to the audience – whilst reading the news (Scannell, 1996: 14). Such objects function as part of a set of mechanisms that operate to construct not only a one-to-many but also a one-to-one relationship between a television performer and the viewer at home. Where felicitous, these mechanisms – not only the newsreader's direct gaze to camera, but also, for instance, the use of personal pronouns which seek to establish a connection between an 'I' who is speaking and a 'you' who is watching and listening – work to establish an interactive or 'discourse' space (Morse, 1985: 5) operating across the distance between the *there* of the broadcaster and the *here* of reception. The talk in this space is necessarily 'immediate': whatever the time, past or present, when such utterances are produced, it is always and inevitably *now* when they are received. To be directly addressed by television is thus to be enlisted into a relationship where someone is speaking to *me now*. As I watch, lips move, and talk is produced in the moment of my attending to it; I appear to be engaging in an immediate interaction-at-a-distance, irrespective of when the talk was actually produced (Morse, 1983: 63). As Ellis writes:

> The broadcast TV image has the effect of immediacy. It is as though the TV image is a 'live' image, transmitted and received in the same moment that it is produced.

For British broadcast TV, with its tight schedules and fear of controversy, this has not been true for a decade. Only news and sport are routinely live transmissions. However, the notion that broadcast TV is live still haunts the medium; even more so does the sense of the immediacy of the image. The immediacy of the broadcast TV image does not just lie in the presumption that it is live, it lies more in the relations that the image sets up for itself. Immediacy is the effect of the directness of the TV image, the way in which it constitutes itself and its viewers as held in a relation of co-present intimacy.

(Ellis, 1992: 132)

This immediacy effect, furthermore, is enhanced by the propensity, in certain genres at least, to shoot events 'as live'. Watching material shot in one continuous take, we not only always and inevitably receive the message in the *now* of our apprehension of it, but also receive a message whose duration corresponds with the duration of the encounter. Such material would appear to carry with it a promise of 'liveness', at least in the limited sense that what we are watching is advertising itself as relatively raw, as playing itself out before our eyes without institutional intervention. As Scannell argues,

the liveness of broadcasting, its sense of existing in real time – the time of the programme corresponding to the time of its reception – is a pervasive effect of the medium.

(Scannell, 1991: 1)

This argument seems reasonably plausible, but shifts the ground away from the notion of immediacy as a concrete set of temporal and spatial relations between television and its audience; and it is, furthermore, subject to the same kinds of caveats that typified the earlier discussions. By no means all communication on television seeks to constitute itself discursively in this way. Some channels, for instance, particularly in an era of narrowcasting and increasingly specialized audience targeting, largely or entirely relinquish direct modes of address. Caldwell (1995: 31) discusses the case of certain 'satellite system broadcasts in Asia and Africa', where 'aged entertainment products' dominate the output and there may be little or no enactment of an immediate encounter between television performer and viewer or, indeed, of a real-time encounter. Dedicated film and pornography channels, which may or may not feature (live? recorded?) continuity announcements between segments, serve as a further example. Television, in these cases, appears to have dispensed with the communicative mechanisms which have been identified as ontologically primary by writers such as Ellis, creating distinct difficulties for the notion that the liveness effect is a pervasive feature of television output. We may wish, rather, to adopt Morse's position here, who suggests that television switches incessantly between the discourse space of a seemingly direct encounter between the television performer and the viewer and a 'story space' in which it is a third-person narration, in a realm separate in time and space, which is on offer (Morse, 1985: 5). This shifts even this part of the discussion from a consideration of the phenomenology of television as whole to a more partial consideration of the way in which immediacy is performed in particular non-fictional genres. The argument for television's 'immediacy effect', for its always and invariably constituting itself around 'a particular regime of representation that stresses the immediacy and co-presence of the TV representation' (Ellis, 1992: 137) would then appear to fall by the wayside.

3.5   The Immanence of Liveness

The arguments in the previous section suggest that it is difficult to sustain the thesis that television is ontologically live. Some arguments, as we have seen, turn out to be a question of the way the apparatus functions, or of the instantaneity of transmission and reception; others have to do with the communicative dynamic between television and its audience. None, it would seem, have much to say about the notion that television is *necessarily* immediate, if we understand by immediacy the simultaneity of an event and its reception elsewhere.

It would appear, then, to be difficult to mount a plausible argument in favour of the ontological immediacy of television; and we should not be all that surprised that this turns out to be the case. At the end of Chapter 2, I argued for the importance of drawing a distinction between the *affordances* of a particular technological form (the uses to which it will permit itself to be put) and its essential nature. When we come to consider the various electronic media one by one, it rapidly becomes apparent that each has its own set of affordances and its own ontological structure. As I argued in the previous chapter, for example, the telephone – answering devices apart – necessarily affords encounters which are not only instantaneous but also immediate. Other characteristics of its mode of operation, however, appear less likely to be ontologically given. Like other telecommunication systems, telephony affords to its users remote encounters, interactions between individuals who are not currently inhabiting the same place. A little thought will make it clear, however, that this is not a *necessary* characteristic of telephone conversations. The development of mobile phone technology has made it possible for individuals to phone each other from different regions of the same place (a club; a shopping centre; a large-scale public event) in order to track each other down, and indeed to ring or text each other in the same room in order to pass on information or note each other's numbers. Similarly, whilst the everyday norms of telephone usage would lead us to expect that conversations will take place between individuals who are directing their conversation specifically at each other, this would once again not appear to be ontologically given. As the discussion in Chapter 1 made clear, the telephone was originally designed as a broadcast medium rather than as a point-to-point device; the possibility always exists, therefore, that it can be used not only to deliver an interaction with a specific other, but also to effect an encounter with an unspecified collectivity of individuals. The conference call functionality of modern telephone systems would appear to restore some aspects of this original broadcast function, inasmuch as it makes it possible for me to interact simultaneously with a group of people, some of whom may be unknown to me and indeed unspecified. On a larger scale, the live broadcasting of music on mobile phones performs a similar function.[4]

Instantaneity and immediacy apart, then, an examination of the communicative affordances of the telephone rapidly begins to demonstrate that few of its characteristics are ontologically given. It begins to emerge, furthermore, that the uses to which the telephone can be put have altered over time. Many of the taken-for-granted features of telephony, in other words, are historically constituted, and are subject to change as individuals come to use them for different purposes and/or as new technological development adds new functionalities which bring new interactive possibilities in their wake.

What about television? Like all electronic forms of communication, television is capable of providing its audience with an encounter with an elsewhere which is both instantaneous and immediate. Like the telephone, furthermore, television permits individuals to address distant others; but whereas the broadcasting capability of telephony has become peripheral to its central function as a mechanism for one-to-one interactions, television readily constitutes itself as a system for the address of the many by the few. Radio, of course, also possesses the same broadcasting capability as television; but television delivers the distant world not just through sound but also through the modality of sight, allowing the audience not only to listen in on a representation of what is going on elsewhere but also to witness it visually. To watch television is to be in the grip of an apparatus which appears to be able to deliver the distant world into the audience's immediate vicinity and which promises, furthermore, that it can do so in the moment of that world's unfolding.

As with telephony, little of this capability is ontologically given. Television's address to the many is supplemented by a number of other circuits of communication, by no means all of them directed at non-specific individuals. Just as the talk on radio can shift momentarily from a generalized and non-specific address to its audience to an individualized and personalized interpellation of an individual or individuals (Montgomery, 1986), so television is clearly capable of singling out one or more members of the audience at home for point-to-point communication. Television's default mode of address, as I said in Chapter 1, is what Scannell (2000: 9) refers to as a 'for-anyone-as-someone structure': an address that is non-specific as to its target, but nevertheless invariably appears to be 'for me'. Nevertheless, a number of non-fiction genres give rise to multiple communicative circuits, shifting from moment to moment between non-specific and specific forms of address. The programme *Babestation* on British satellite television, for instance, features semi-undressed women who perform in a number of windows on the screen for individuals who phone or text to ask them to carry out particular kinds of activities: blow a kiss at the screen, waggle and/or reveal a particular part of their anatomy and so on. In another window on the screen, scrolling text messages from individual viewers appear, either again requesting the presenters to carry out particular sexual gestures or

---

[4]See http://www.guardian.co.uk/arts/news/story/0,11711,1341956,00.html (accessed 10 August 2005).

directly addressing the presenters in fairly explicitly sexual terms. Presenters frequently reply to such requests and comments with a direct address to the individual concerned. The same holds true, *mutatis mutandis*, for phone-ins on live television programmes, where the presenter or a guest expert will alternate between a for-anyone-as-someone address to the audience at home and a direct one-to-one interaction with the caller. Live television, in fact, can present the viewer with a dazzling array of communicative circuits, shifting its address from moment to moment from one segment of the audience to another. *Noel's House Party*, for example, a live Saturday evening show which ran for several years on British television, would alternate in quick succession between the following sets of addressees: a studio guest or guests; the studio audience; the audience at home; Noel's accomplice who was setting up a prank at a distant location; the subjects of the prank. The last three of these communicative circuits ran between the studio and a simultaneous elsewhere; all of them were accompanied by a direct gaze (to camera; to an individual or individuals in the studio; to a monitor) which rendered the target of address transparent from one moment to the next.

The for-anyone-as-someone structure of television, then, is not ontologically given: whilst it is clearly the dominant mode of address, certain genres of television – and of live television in particular – also give rise to a number of other communicative circuits which can directly address an individual or individuals in the studio, down-the-line at a remote location or at home.

Other aspects of television's communicative regime similarly permit of exceptions that make it clear that little is ontologically given. Just as telephony – in the form of mobile phones and indeed of multiple extension lines in the same office – is capable of delivering communication between co-present as well as remote individuals, so television can transmit images locally as well as across distance. The on-the-scene events commentator with a monitor at hand which displays what he or she can perfectly well see with a naked eye, the stadium audience who have at their disposal a video wall rendition of the action that is unfolding around them even as it is being broadcast to elsewhere, the down-the-line news correspondent in a remote location monitoring their own performance on a small television screen even as they deliver it; all of these are examples of television's ability to bounce events back to the vicinity in which they are taking place in the real time of their occurrence so that they can be watched in the place where they are happening. *Noel's House Party* featured some particularly interesting examples of this phenomenon: via a hidden camera implanted in a television set, the programme was able to produce sudden candid camera shots of a family watching the programme at home, caught on live television in the very moment of consumption like nocturnal animals transfixed by oncoming car headlights. Rightly celebrated at its inception for its ability to transmit images from remote locales – hence its name, meaning *vision at a distance* – broadcast television can also afford its users, under a limited range of circumstances, a mediated encounter with their own locality. Such examples do not represent the bulk of the viewing experience; but they may be enough to persuade us that we cannot talk about television as *necessarily* remote, though we might want to argue that the delivery of sounds and images across distance is clearly one of its key *affordances*.

The liveness of television falls into the same category. As this chapter has amply demonstrated, not all of television is immediate; indeed at certain key stages in its historical development, full liveness – instantaneous or near-instantaneous transmission of an event in the moment of its unfolding – has been relegated to a distinctly marginal role in television's output. Immediacy, like many other aspects of television's communicative regime, is thus not ontologically given; it is, however, a key affordance. The following will serve as a preliminary example.

It is 1.30 a.m. on 31 May 2005, and I switch on my television. Some 300 channels are available for me to watch. The majority of these are showing films, or repeats of old television programmes, or recordings of sporting events; in some cases the as-live look to camera and direct address of a presenter makes it difficult for me to be sure whether I am looking at a live transmission or not. Some forty of these channels appear to be unmistakably live, either because of real-time interactive features (home shopping channels where the individuals purchasing items are displayed on a crawl at the bottom of the screen and the number of items remaining is continually updated in a further window; game channels where callers are phoning in to win money; soft porn stations with incoming texts displayed on a vertical scroll) or because the programmes bear the legend 'live' on the screen (24-hour rolling news channels; live overnight coverage of reality shows; live sports from some other part of the world where the majority of the population are still awake). One channel features something which is at first a little hard to grasp. The Soundtrack Channel is showing a programme which it calls *STC Live*, but what I can see on the screen is a sequence of clips from Hollywood films on current release, unattended as far as I can tell by continuity announcements or any other kind of institutional intervention in the moment of transmission and reception. How, then, can this be live? The answer would appear to lie in the crawl at the bottom of the screen, where a space has been made available for viewers to interact with each other by text. These texts emanate from a multiplicity of simultaneous places in which individuals are encountering each other through the mediation of the screen. *STC Live*, then, if it is live, is live purely by virtue of the real-time relationships it facilitates between members of the audience; to the extent that it produces immediate encounters, these are encounters between one audience member and another, available to be viewed in the real time of their unfolding by anyone who is tuning in, whether a participant in the exchanges or not.

This somewhat marginal example from late-night satellite viewing has an important point to make, which is that liveness is an *immanent feature* of all transmissions, all of the time. Even a programme composed of pre-recorded material and entirely stripped of any kind of overtly 'live' institutional voice has the potential to include, as one of its communicative mechanisms, an interactive circuit that permits an immediate encounter between remote sites. Immediacy is not, in other words, simply an affordance of television in the way that, say, broadcast communication is an affordance of telephony; immediacy is central to the work that television does, insofar as it is at all moments a potential feature of its output. Consider once again the events of the morning of 11 September 2001 on American television. Whether the magazine programmes at 8.48 a.m. were at that moment running a live studio segment or a pre-recorded feature made no odds; all moved instantly to offer their audiences an immediate encounter with an event whose level of newsworthiness overrode all considerations of scheduling. This event could be brought to the audience in the moment of its unfolding because liveness perpetually underpins the flow of broadcasting, always available as an option because the instantaneity of transmission and reception renders it a constant possibility. Whether television, in a particular segment on a particular day, opts to realize that potential or not is beside the point: immediacy resides in the medium as a continual promise, forever on the brink of emergence.

That television also manipulates this promise of liveness for its own ends makes no difference. To say that liveness is an immanent feature of television's mode of operation is not to deny that it has a key ideological function to play in the way that television presents itself to its audience; nor does it rule out the possibility that it can be manifested as a set of stylistic options which may bear little relationship to the actual spatio-temporal status of the image at a given moment.[5] It is, however, to suggest that the claim that liveness is 'the very definition of television' (Heath and Skirrow, 1977: 53) may not be as extravagant as it seems. If liveness is not ontologically given, it is nevertheless latent in the medium at all moments and under all sets of circumstances. Why this might be of interest is something that the rest of the book will set itself to explore.

---

[5] See Caldwell, 1995; Feuer, 1983.

4

Time and the Live Event

Why should liveness matter? ... Because events only happen in the present. In
a word, gambling.

(Peters, 2001: 719)

4.1 Liveness and Immediacy

If it is true that much of 'live' television is not truly or fully live, then it is equally
true that the majority of television programmes are not live at all.[1] The ratio of
fully live to non-live broadcasting would be likely to increase, of course, on a day
when a major catastrophe or disaster is dominating output on several channels.
Even in such a case, however, chances are that the majority of satellite channels
would still be relaying their standard mix of films, soaps, sitcoms, dramas and
other pre-recorded material.

Liveness as a phenomenon of the schedules, however, stubbornly refuses
to go away. Certain events, certain genres appear to demand it. The large-
scale media event (weddings, funerals, processions, national and international
sports matches, ceremonial occasions, telethons, election nights and the like), the
24-hour surveillance of the goings-on in reality television set-ups, early-morning
and late-night magazine shows, news programmes and rolling news, shopping
and gaming channels, one-off episodes of long-running television drama series
which are shot and transmitted even as they are performed, all of these appear to
require it as a felicity condition that they should deliver and be seen to deliver
some simultaneous elsewhere to a remote audience.[2]

Certain kinds of live events, moreover, are still capable of attracting large
audiences, bucking the general trend towards narrowcasting and niche markets.
It is possible, for instance, given the right event, to garner a domestic audience
in Britain of anything between 20 million (the England versus Portugal match
in the Euro 2004 football championship) and 31 million (the funeral of Princess
Diana in 1997);[3] and whilst neither of these figures can compare to the 600
million around the world who watched the first landing on the moon in 1969,[4]

---

[1] An earlier draft of some of the material in this chapter originally appeared in Marriott (1997).

[2] On felicity conditions, see Austin (2005).

[3] Figures taken respectively from the *Guardian*, 5 July 2005, and an ITN press release,
8 September 1997.

[4] http://outreach.atnf.csiro.au/about/achievements/parkes/ (accessed 15 January 2006).

they are certainly enough to indicate that liveness, at the right time and in the right context, is still a considerable draw.

In addition, live television characteristically makes much of itself. The liveness of particular broadcasts is frequently highlighted well in advance in trailers and promotional material; and the programmes themselves sometimes repeatedly foreground, in moments of high self-reflexivity, the central significance of immediacy to the broadcast.

We saw one instance of this in the previous chapter ('And this is live, by the way, it's really gonna happen at 9 o'clock', taken from a live breakfast show on the morning of 11 September 2001). For a more sustained set of examples we can turn to a brief consideration of one particular genre, the live nature-watch programme.

Such programmes, when they turn up in the schedules, tend to occur at regular intervals over a period of some days or weeks. *Springwatch*, for instance, was broadcast twice a day over a three-week period between 2004 and 2006 in Britain, in each case featuring a number of live 'visits' to nest sites, badger setts and the like, where the machinery of live transmission made it possible to watch what was going on *right now* in a host of elsewheres. That the liveness of the material was seen as a central attraction of the programmes seems undeniable, judging, at least, by the presenters' utterances. As the programmes repeatedly shifted from fully live material to pre-recorded segments and back again, so the presenters reiterated wherever possible the immediacy of the images the audience was looking at or was about to see ('This is live'; 'Let's go live'; 'We're back live I think now').

Bird in the Nest, a forerunner of *Springwatch*, similarly constituted itself around this discourse of immediacy, going out of its way again and again to emphasize the liveness of the broadcast. *Bird in the Nest*'s several daily visits to nest sites regularly stressed the immediacy of what was on offer (as one presenter said, correcting another who had just informed the audience that they were looking at little owls, 'they're *live* little owls'), and also made repeated references to the *nowness* of the image. Here are some examples, taken from the various daily visits to the nest sites:

1.   And that's coming back **live now** – there they are **live** again.
2.   We're back **live** again **now**.
3.   A   That's them **live**.
     B   That's them **live, at the moment** they're sleeping.
4.   And we can actually see that family **right now live**, if we go over to Peter Holden over in the birdmobile over there.

It is not difficult to see why nature watch programmes such as *Springwatch* and *Bird in the Nest* make much both of the liveness of the broadcast and of the immediacy which that entails ('We're back live again *now*'). A central motivation for watching such programmes, presumably, is that they offer the viewer the opportunity to see nature 'as it is' and 'as it is happening'. Hence the mapping of the schedule onto the diurnal rhythms of the birds: it is not so much a case of appropriate programming for the needs of the audience at a particular time of day, as of scheduling the live episodes so that the daily routines of the birds can be observed as they happen. The impact of such programmes depends on seeing what the birds are doing *as they do it*; to watch it after the event is to be stripped of the enchantment which the programmes offer by virtue of their ability to bring hidden places into the immediate vicinity of the audience in the moment of their unfolding.

To watch such footage at a later date is to be placed in a fundamentally different relation to the event. The extract below, from *Bird in the Nest*, clearly represents, as before, a presenter who stands in an immediate relation to the events that are transpiring in the nest box:

5. We're back live now, and as you can see, there's only three there, but there are four, and I expect you'd like to know where the fourth one is. By a miracle of computerized gadgetry we can show you. You can see that sort of perspex panel has arrived there and you see there's a little corridor leading to the outside and it's because it's in a box that the baby's able to get to that entrance. If it were nesting in a tree as they would often be it would have to climb up and it wouldn't be able to do that yet.

In this utterance, as with the earlier examples, the presenter reiterates the liveness and the *nowness* of the image ('We're back *live now*'). Several other characteristics mark this discourse as live in their enactment of an immediate relationship between the presenter, the audience and the event. The utterance is, first, in the present tense ('We're back live now'; 'there *are* four'; 'there's a little corridor leading to the outside'), indicating that the events under discussion are happening *right now*; second, it directly addresses the remote viewer ('as *you* can see'; 'I expect *you*'d like to know'; 'we can show *you*') as a witness of the events unfolding in the real time of transmission. Moreover, what is there to be witnessed is marked as intersubjectively available through the use of deictic expressions which directly index some element of what is jointly available to both presenter and viewer *right now* on their screens. When the presenter indicates the nest box to the audience by pointing out that they 'can see that sort of perspex panel has arrived there', he is presupposing that they can see exactly what he can see (the nest box, on their screens) in the same moment in which he is both seeing it and pointing it out to them. The presenter's utterance, in other words, works to construct the kind of 'discourse space' (Morse, 1985: 5) which was briefly discussed in Chapter 3, which is characterized by the offer of a real-time connection between the 'I' of television and the 'you' of the viewer, located in the simultaneous moment in which the event, the speaking of the event and the reception of the event are all transpiring.

The presenter's description of the nest box – of what is going on *now*, as both presenter and viewer peruse the image – can be instructively compared with a discussion of the same material in an update programme several weeks later:

6. On Monday the adults were still spending a lot of time keeping the chicks warm by tightly brooding them and we only got the odd glance of fluff as they wiggled about. On Tuesday feeding began at about 9.30 and within an hour the chicks had had 25 feeds of worms and moths. Later that night they

started to wander out of the main nest chamber down towards the nest exit. When the first chick disappeared for a full half hour we got worried. Maybe it had fallen out of the nest and maybe out of the tree. But by the wonder of computer graphics we could reveal where it had gone – a corridor – and there it was, quite safe. In fact on Wednesday our infrared cameras revealed just why the chick had ventured into uncharted territory. You see, it's true, the early bird does get the worm. In fact we were quite surprised that these birds caught virtually no small mammals. By the end of the week all hell was breaking loose inside the box when the first feeds arrived. The adults, who incidentally pair for life, were hunting until the early hours to feed their brood ...

This utterance still retains something of the interpersonal flavour of the live original, possibly because the presenter is casting an eye back over the same events that he had originally discussed live. There is still a measure of direct address in the text, insofar as there is a residual 'we' of the programme makers ('*we* got worried'; '*our* infrared cameras') still addressing the 'you' of the audience ('*you* see, the early bird does get the worm'). In other respects, however, the address to the viewer has shifted. The tense is primarily a mixture of the simple past and the pluperfect ('maybe it *had fallen* out of the nest'; 'we could reveal where it *had gone*'), indicating that the events under discussion are no longer transpiring in tandem with his commentary; and the material has been transmuted into a linear narrative with an ordering that places each state of affairs in a chronological relation to the next ('On Monday'; 'On Tuesday'; 'Later that night'; 'By the end of the week'). If the original live event offered the viewer an immediate encounter both with the presenter and with the denizens of the nest box, then the recap places the interaction, vestigial moments of direct address apart, fairly firmly in the 'story space' (Morse, 1985: 5) from which television narrates events that are removed both in time and in space from the *here-and-now* of either presenter or audience.

This sharp set of contrasts between the commentary on the live event and on the recap is by no means limited to this one programme, or to one genre alone. A similar set of features emerges whenever we come to consider a parallel set of circumstances. Here, for example, is an extract from a live snooker match:

7.   A   Well that's the worse shot he's played throughout the break. Didn't really get high enough. He could try and split them but he's such a good long potter I think it'll be a long blue into one of the corner pockets. Needs it to run a little. So now blue into the yellow pocket, and if he gets this he will be pushing the pink towards the centre pocket. Well the blue's there.

     B   Great chance now.

     A   Yes and look for the roar if this pink and black goes in. Slow down. Well this would be a pressure shot to win a frame but for a 147 I promise you the pressure has got to be the greatest ever.

B   He's got it. Stephen Hendry makes it the third 147 maximum in Crucible history and takes a bonus of £147,000.

As in (5), the commentator here makes similar reference to the present moment of the act of speech ('So *now* blue into the yellow pocket'; 'Great chance *now*') and again demonstratively indicates several of the elements that are jointly available to both commentator and viewer on the screen ('*that*'s the worse shot he's played throughout the break'; 'if he gets *this* he will be pushing the pink towards the centre pocket'; '*this* would be a pressure shot to win a frame'). The same presupposition of an interpersonal connection between commentator and remote viewer is present too ('*I* promise *you* the pressure has got to be the greatest ever'). This invocation of the relationship between the speaker and the hearer again locates the discourse firmly within the realms of both the intersubjective (the discursive formation of an interpersonal relationship between the speaker and the hearer) and the subjective (the explicit presence in the text of the speaking subject). Speaker-subjectivity is further emphasized by the frequent expression of the commentator's own opinions. The commentator 'think[s] it'll be a long blue into one of the corner pockets' and is of the opinion that the player 'needs it to run a little'; and goes on, throughout the rest of the discourse, to intersperse brief descriptions of what has happened ('Well the blue's there') with more lengthy prognostications on likely and possible outcomes ('if he gets this he will be pushing the pink towards the centre pocket'; 'look for the roar if this pink and black goes in'; 'this would be a pressure shot to win a frame').

Such opinions are generally hedged in one of a number of ways, adding an air of tentativity to the assurance with which predictions about the future are made. Direct expressions of futurity, for example, are either preceded by a verb of mental state to emphasize that what follows is conjecture rather than foreknowledge ('I *think* it'll be a long blue into one of the corner pockets') or they appear in the main clause of a conditional sentence to mark their non-factual status ('*if* he gets this he *will* be pushing the pink towards the centre pocket').

If we compare this material with an extract from a news report later on the same day, then the differences are again clear:

8.   Fifteen reds later, just six balls stood between him and his ultimate goal. With the yellow, green and brown safely tucked away, he then played a delightful pot to sink the blue. So much was riding on the next two shots. If he was nervous, he didn't show it. The crowd were on tenterhooks, while all Jimmy White could do, kept away from the table for so long by Hendry's brilliance, was watch.

The only tense found in this extract is the simple past ('just six balls *stood* between him and his ultimate goal'; 'he then *played* a delightful pot'); and tense apart, there are no deictic expressions, and no interpersonal references to either the producer of the text (the 'I' of (7)) or its intended receiver. The news report also fundamentally lacks the element of emotional attachment to the action at hand which is so noticeable in the live commentary, where the speaker, in the heat of the moment, exhorts the unhearing player to 'slow down'. Furthermore, the report is clearly produced with the benefit of hindsight, rather than from the lugubrious perspective of a commentator watching the action unfold in real time and hedging his bets. '[T]he worse shot he's played throughout the break' in (7) has been transmuted, in (8), to an admiring reference to the safe tucking away of the 'yellow, green and brown', and the laconic 'Well the blue's there' is transformed into the enthusiastic 'delightful pot to sink the blue'. Finally the news report, like the *Bird in the Nest* update programme, narrates the story in chronological order, with one state of affairs following on from another ('With the yellow, green and brown safely tucked away, he *then* played a delightful pot to sink the blue'). During the live commentary, by contrast, events were described in terms of their relationship to the present moment: they happened *before* the present moment ('Didn't really get high enough'), *at* or *around* it ('Well the blue's there') or, potentially, *after* it ('He could try and split them'; 'if he gets this he will be pushing the pink towards the centre pocket').

The difference between these two examples could, of course, be down to the relatively formal tone customarily associated with news reports, with their projection of facticity and their overtly disinterested institutional voice (Montgomery, 2006). The same contrasts turn up, however, wherever one encounters both a simultaneous and a subsequent narration of the same events. This shows up particularly clearly in the next set of examples, taken from a BBC Sports Review of the Year broadcast. In each case, the voiceover that accompanies the pre-recorded actuality footage gives way at certain points to the voices of the commentators on the original live soundtrack, allowing us to compare the two varieties directly:

9. But for Britain the championship highlight was the performance of Jonathan Edwards. Round one of the triple jump. OH IT'S HUGE, IT'S MASSIVE, MY GOODNESS THAT IS FANTASTIC, AND IT'S LEGAL. ONE POINT THREE METRES PER SECOND. THE WORLD RECORD IS 17 METRES 98. OH MY GOODNESS GRACIOUS ME. 18 METRES 16. IT'S LEGAL, IT'S A WORLD RECORD FOR GREAT BRITAIN AND JONATHAN EDWARDS. What Bob Beamon had once done in long jump Edwards was now doing in his event. New dimensions. OH IT'S A TOUGH ACT TO FOLLOW BUT HE'S DONE IT AGAIN. IT IS EXACTLY SIXTY FEET AND ONE QUARTER OF AN INCH. JONATHAN EDWARDS HAS MADE HISTORY AGAIN.[5]

10. Boris Becker was back, explosive, exciting, often for wife Barbara excruciating, but overall exceptional. OH EXTRAORDINARY. He won the five-set quarter final thriller against Cédric Pioline. Next it was Agassi. And for the first set and a half it was all André. OH BRILLIANT. But from there the German began to turn it around. And to most of the crowd's delight he was close to victory. Becker had made his point, but would it prove to be his destiny, ten years on from his first victory? It wasn't to be. In the final, Becker was tired physically and mentally, never producing

---

[5] Original live commentary in upper case.

his best. Sampras as always was outstanding and continued his domination at the greatest championship. Sampras had the trophy finally, Becker had the centre-court cheers.

As before, we can see the contrast here between the highly subjective and excitable style of the live commentators ('my goodness that is fantastic'; 'oh my goodness gracious me'; 'oh extraordinary'; 'oh brilliant') and the measured delivery of the narrators in the studio. And again we find different sets of tenses: the simple past and the pluperfect, predominantly, for the voiceovers ('the German *began* to turn it around'; 'Becker *had made* his point), and the present and the present perfect for the live commentary ('it'*s* huge, it'*s* massive'; 'he'*s done* it again'). As with (6) and (8), too, events are recounted in a largely chronological order, particularly in the final extract where the viewer is taken step-by-step through the action as it took place, with the exception of the rhetorical question and answer on the likelihood of Becker's winning the championship, added with the benefit of hindsight ('would it prove to be his destiny, ten years on from his first victory? It wasn't to be').

4.2   The Uncertainty of the Moment

The extracts in the previous section demonstrate a clear distinction between the kind of commentary that would appear to be appropriate to an individual describing events as they happen versus the discourse that ensues after the event. Live commentary, characteristically, positions the audience as a direct witness to a situation which is unfolding on television, offering the viewer an immediate encounter both with the commentator and with the event. The commentary on events that occurred earlier, by contrast, offers an overview of the event which is largely stripped of both subjective and intersubjective elements and which imposes a chronological order on the material on display.

As the brief discussion about story versus discourse spaces suggests, the differences between these two modes of talk can be summarized in terms of a distinction between a narrative and a non-narrative mode of description. Many such distinctions exist: Benveniste (1971) differentiates what he calls 'story' and 'discourse', Weinrich (1970) draws a distinction between 'narrative' and 'discursive' speech situations and Lyons (1977, 1982) between a 'historical' and an 'experiential' mode of description.

These sets of binary distinctions all have in common that they set a reasonably objective mode of talk against a basically subjective one. Lyons (1982: 117), for example, comments that his dichotomy 'emphasizes the distinction between the relative objectivity of straightforward narration and the greater subjectivity that is associated with the description of personal experience'.

For Benveniste this subjectivity manifests itself in the fundamentally inter-personal dimension which characterizes his category of 'discourse'. As Morse (1985: 3) comments:

> *Story* and *discourse* ... are two planes of language, the former suppressing subjectivity in order to refer to an objective and separate realm of space and time inhabited by

others (he, she and it), the latter a plane of subjectivity in which a person, 'I', adopts responsibility for an utterance and calls for intersubjective relations with a 'you' in the here and now.

Underlying this distinction is a contrast in temporal perspective. Narrative or historical descriptions do not only involve speaker objectivity; they are also likely to involve the recounting of events as if they occurred successively at some point prior to the moment of speech. In experiential accounts, by contrast, events will be talked about as if they are occurring at or around the moment of speech, so that situations will be described 'not in their successivity in relation to one another' but 'as having just occurred, if they are momentary events ... or as extending on either side of the moment of utterance if, as is usually the case, they are not momentary events' (Lyons, 1982: 119).

Lyons explicitly relates his dichotomy of historical and experiential to the distinction we examined in Chapter 2 between 'static' and 'dynamic' ways of talking about time (Lyons, 1977: 688). Viewed from a static perspective, time is organized in a linear fashion, with one event following on from or preceding another; viewed dynamically, the relation of events to each other shifts as the speaker enters into an ever-new *now*-moment.

This notion of dynamic time can, in turn, be usefully understood with reference to the notion of the *phenomenological now* which I briefly addressed in Chapter 2. All our encounters with the world necessarily take place at this *now-moment*: just as the place where I am can only, under any set of circumstances, be *here*, so the moment is always *now*. This is equally the case whether I am engaged in an interaction with others who are currently inhabiting the same place as me or individuals at a remote location, and is equally so whether I am interacting with some element of the world which is transpiring *now* (the rain outside my window; my hands tapping on the keyboard in front of me) or something which transpired in some previous moment but was captured in a form which makes it possible for me to peruse it later (a printed book or newspaper; a text sent to me an hour ago on my mobile phone; an email sent yesterday). Ineluctably, invariably, I encounter events from the *here-and-now* of my bodily engagement with the world. Whatever I am doing, the moment in which I am doing it is the generative *now*, the *now* of lived experience.

Our experience of this generative now, as both Husserl and Bergson argue, cannot be reduced to the instant in which the moment perpetually unfolds itself, 'the instantaneous which dies and is born again endlessly' (Bergson, 1911: 211). Rather, the experiential present has, as Bergson puts it, one foot in the past and another in the future:

What is, for me, the present moment? The essence of time is that it goes by; time already gone by is in the past, and we call the present the instant in which it goes past ... No doubt there is an ideal present – a pure conception, the indivisible limit which separates past from future. But the real, concrete, live present – that of which I speak when I speak of my present perception – that present necessarily occupies a duration. Where then is this duration placed? Is it on the nearer or on the further side of the mathematical point which I determine ideally when I think of the present instant? Quite evidently, it is both on this side and on that, and what I call 'my present' has one foot in my past and another in my future. In my past, first, because 'the moment in which I am speaking is already far from me'; in my future, next, because this moment is impending over my future: it is to the future that I am tending ... The psychical state, then, that I call 'my present', must be both a perception of the immediate past and a determination of the immediate future.

(Bergson, 1988: 137)

Experientially, then, we inhabit a 'specious' or 'thickened' present (Kern, 1983: 83), which extends perceptually into the immediate past and anticipates the immediate future, and which involves a continuous 'sinking back' of the now-point and its replacement with a new now:

the duration of the sound apprehended in the now ... constantly sinks back into the past and an ever new point of duration enters into the now or is now ... the expired duration recedes from the actual now-point ... and moves back into an ever more 'distant' past, and so on.

(Husserl, 1964: 46)

Both Husserl and Bergson stress that the passage of time involves a continuous creation of the new. For Bergson, the present is 'simply *what is being made*' (1988: 149), the 'continuous elaboration of the absolutely new' (1911: 11), so that reality is 'a ceaseless upspringing of something new, which has no sooner arisen to make the present than it has already fallen back into the past' (1911: 49); and for Husserl (1964: 86), similarly, 'above all, the now-moment is characterized as the new. The now, just sinking away, is no longer the new, but that which is shoved aside by the new'.

Bergson in particular, in his notion of *durée* or 'duration', develops the idea of the universe as a 'continuity of becoming' (1988: 139) in which both we and the universe 'endure' (1911: 11). In a Bergsonian model, time is thus 'constituted in emergence' (Adam, 1990: 24). All events which are in time are emergent events, and all acts – whether human or not – are emergent acts, manifesting themselves in a 'present which is always beginning again' (Bergson, 1988: 139) and which can never repeat itself.

It follows from this discussion that all human activity must possess the property of emergence. Every occurrence, every thing that we do or think or say or hear is delivered into a fresh moment of time, a now-moment which has never occurred before and which can never occur again. And it is from the perspective of emergence that we can understand the use of deictic expressions in the live snooker commentary. When the commentator says that 'if he gets *this* he will be pushing the pink towards the centre pocket', or that '*this* would be a pressure shot to win a frame', he intends by the use of the demonstrative expression *this* two different snooker shots, each shot in turn coming into being in the emergent *now* of the commentary. The first occurrence of 'now' in the same example – 'So *now* blue into the yellow pocket' – similarly has a different referent from the second occurrence ('Great chance *now*'), the first being uttered at the moment when the player is about to attempt the blue ball and the second when he is going for the pink. Live commentary is deictic because, like other experiential discourse, it involves the identification and location of elements in an ever-unfolding and ever-novel present moment.

The subjectivity of a speaker perpetually poised on the edge of unknowable events also reveals itself in the expression of personal opinions and of conjectures – frequently hedged – about what is to come. In the relatively unpredictable set of circumstances which govern much live commentary, the foreshadowing of possible futures will typically pass over, first into an examination of the present and then into the immediate past. Consider the next extract, taken from the live commentary on a bowls match, which begins as the player prepares to take his next shot, continues as the bowl proceeds down the green and concludes as it reaches its target:

11.   Well Mervyn, if he can make a contact with his own nearest blue bowl and punch out the nearest McMahon bowl, could establish a set and match winning lie – he's running after it – he rather likes it – he's thereabouts – he's got it.

The presence in the opening stages of this utterance of a conditional sentence ('Mervyn, *if* he can make a contact with his own nearest blue bowl ... could establish a set and match winning lie'), indicates a speaker balanced on the edge of a yet-to-unfold event and speculating about what is to come. In the 'thickened' present of speech, the commentator then follows the player down the green ('he's running after it') and then pronounces, in a tone of steadily rising excitement, on the outcome, moving from a present tense for the description of events that are still unfolding as he speaks ('he rather likes it'; 'he's thereabouts') to the use of the perfect to signal the conclusion of an event whose reverberations can still be felt in the present ('he's got it').

4.3   The Emergent Present: Derren Brown's Russian Roulette

Not all live television talk is in an experiential mode. Live news broadcasts, for instance, switch between a discourse space characterized by direct gaze to camera and direct address to the viewer and a story space in which the news is narrated in a historical mode. All live television talk, however, whether experiential or not, is constituted in emergence. Even the pre-scripted historical coverage of pre-recorded actuality footage involves the newsreader in the production of talk at the emergent *now* of the live transmission. This is the case because *all* linguistic utterances, whether spoken or written, are produced at the deictic zero-point, the phenomenological *now*; necessarily so, if we accept Levinson's formulation that 'now' can be understood to mean 'the time at which the speaker is producing the utterance containing *now*' (1983: 73). Even non-live talk, on this account, must originally have been generated in the *now* of the speaker's uttering it. Whether the talk on television is being produced in the same moment in which the audience encounter it, or was produced some minutes, days, weeks, months or years earlier, it can only have been uttered in the generative *now* in which all human activity must take place.

Live talk, however, speaks into a *shared* emergent present, at least from the point of view of the message producer. Whether viewers choose to video the broadcast for subsequent consumption or whether they watch it as it is transmitted, the speaker producing live talk at the generative *now* will treat the moment as shared: as one broadcaster puts it, 'It's something quite remarkable. There is an awareness that the red light is on and that what is going out of that tube is ... coming out at the other end somewhere immediately' (McAnally, Wilson and Norris, 1993: 19).

All television talk thus speaks into an ever-new and unpredictable present moment; and live talk, in particular, speaks into a present moment in which the utterance, the reception of the utterance and the event-in-the-world are all transpiring simultaneously. When a presenter points out a perspex panel that 'has arrived' in the nest box 'there', or a commentator exhorts a viewer to 'look for the roar if this pink and black goes in', they are able to do so because of the immediacy and simultaneity which live television brings in its wake. At such moments, the commentator, the viewer and the unfolding event all endure in the same present. To indicate demonstratively some element in the nest box or on the snooker table is to point out to the viewer something that is mutually available *right now* as it takes place both in the world and on the screen in the intersubjective *now* of the live broadcast.

This relationship can be considered both from the point of view of individuals who speak the event as it transpires – presenters, commentators and the like – and from the point of view of the audience who encounter the event in one of the multiplicity of remote locales to which it is transmitted. The commentator, as we saw in the previous section, is perpetually poised on the edge of the new, shifting in turn from the anticipation of what is to come to the delineation of what is transpiring at the *now* of speech and then on to the retrospective examination of what has taken place, before potentially beginning the cycle again. For the viewer, this kind of foreshadowing and then shadowing of the potential and actual consequences of unfolding acts is one of the principal pleasures of liveness; so much so that when a sporting fixture is to be shown at a later time, still accompanied by the original live commentary, viewers of sports round-up programmes or of news broadcasts may be exhorted to 'look away' when results are flashed up on the screen if they do not want to know the outcome in advance. What is lost, when an event is watched with the hindsight of retrospection, is the edge of risk which accompanies the experiencing of emergent reality. Live television, as Zettl (1978: 5) puts it, 'lives off the instantaneousness and uncertainty of the moment very much the way we do in actual life'.

The simultaneity of the event, television's speaking of the event and its remote reception is not, of course, restricted to those genres that feature live commentary. All fully live television, as we saw in Chapter 3, constructs a relationship between simultaneous places through the mediation of the broadcast; all live television offers its audience an encounter with events which are unfolding in the emergent *now* of viewing. All fully live television, therefore, carries with it the promise of an encounter with the *atelic*, with an event that is in the process of coming into being whose end point is not yet determined.[6] It is for this reason that Peters (2001: 719) likens the experience of watching a live broadcast to gambling:

> Why should liveness matter? ... Because events only happen in the present. In a word, gambling ... The past, in some sense, is safe. The present, in contrast, is catastrophic, subject to radical alterations. In a single second a swerve of the steering wheel or a pull of the trigger can change history forever. Possible futures come into being and vanish with every act. In a brief moment the penalty kick is made or missed, a life conceived or taken. All history culminates in the present moment. Of course, the present is rarely so dramatic, but without a live connection its explosive possibility – its danger – is missing. Nothing quite excites like an event about to take place.

Peters draws the reader's attention to Benjamin's view that gambling is a 'phantasmagoria of time' (Peters, 2001: 719); as Benjamin puts it, gambling 'converts time into a narcotic' (Benjamin, 1973: 38). Viewed from the perspective of time-in-emergence, Benjamin's meaning here seems clear: to gamble is to surrender oneself to the addictive thrill of pure duration, to position oneself, momentarily, inside the flux of the moment with its constantly changing horizons of possibility and outcome.

Live television, whether it delivers on this promise or not, offers the same thrill. As Scannell (1996: 84) writes:

> The *liveness* of broadcast coverage is the key to its impact, since it offers the real sense of access to an event in its moment-by-moment unfolding. This *presencing*, this re-presenting of a present occasion to an absent audience, can powerfully produce the effect of being-there, of being involved (caught up) in the here-and-now of the occasion. This being in the moment, especially in its 'unfolding', creates the mood of expectancy: what's happening? what's next?

At its most felicitous, the live event has the power to transport the audience into this moment, a moment which is simultaneous with the *now* of viewing. To be in such a moment is to be lifted out of one's locality with its own thematic concerns and horizons and into the space of the event, whose unfolding reality becomes momentarily thematic for the viewer and whose undetermined outcomes become momentarily horizonal.[7] At such moments, the viewer is plunged into pure duration, where, as Bergson writes, 'our whole personality concentrates itself in a point, or rather a sharp edge, pressed against the future and cutting into it unceasingly' (1911: 212).

This ability to lift the viewer into a moment which is transpiring in a simultaneous elsewhere is one of the key affordances of live television. Consider the stunt that the illusionist, Derren Brown, performed on 5 October 2003 on Channel 4 in Britain. In a programme called *Derren Brown Plays Russian Roulette Live*, Brown selected a member of the public, took him to a remote farmhouse, asked him to load a revolver with a single bullet, and then went on to fire successive rounds at his own head. Having declared that he would only fire away from himself if he believed that the next chamber contained the live ammunition, Brown fired rounds three and four at his temple, putting the gun back down in

---

[6]On telicity, see Vendler (1967).

[7]On the notions of thematic field and horizon, see Schutz 1970; Scbutz & Luckmann 1983.

each case for three or four seconds in between. He then picked up the gun again, held it to his head for a moment and then deliberately extended his arm and fired at a sandbag across the room, bracing himself slightly before he did so. The trigger clicked, but the gun did not go off. The implication seemed clear: Brown had believed that chamber five contained the bullet, but it did not.

Brown now returned the gun to the table in front of him and stared straight ahead across the room. For over a minute he continued to sit in silence, with both hands on the table, immobile apart from steady breathing and an occasional blink of his eyes. Only for one instant – some 25 seconds into the minute – was there any movement, when he raised his right hand a little, apparently changed his mind and returned it to the table. He then sat as before for a further 40 seconds, staring into space in silence. In quick succession he then raised the gun, fired chamber six – empty – at his temple, fired chamber one – the bullet – across the room into the sandbag and rose rapidly to his feet, slamming the gun back down on the table.

James, the member of the public who had loaded the revolver for Brown and had then taken himself off to sit behind a bulletproof screen in the same room, said later that the minute or so in which Brown sat motionless at the table 'seemed to go on for ever'.[8] For the viewer, too, the moment may well have seemed endless. To watch the event subsequently, in a recorded form, is to watch it with the knowledge that at the end of the minute Brown will fire the gun away from himself into the sandbag at the critical juncture, thus saving his own life; to watch it at the time was to be *inside* the event, with no way of predicting how long Brown would sit near-motionless at the table, or what the eventual outcome would be. Brown's apparent paleness and tension, which seemed to reveal itself in the hand which fluttered towards the revolver and subsided again, only intensified for the viewer the feeling of being caught up, *transfixed*, inside the event, entirely absorbed by a now-moment which, impossibly and implausibly, continued to unfold and unfold with no determinable end in sight. At each instant it seemed that Brown must either pick up the gun to resolve the situation or call the whole thing off ('I didn't know if the stunt had gone badly wrong, if it was gonna be cancelled', as James said after the event); at each instant he continued, instead, to sit apparently frozen at the table. As one journalist would write afterwards: 'I sat there rooted to the spot, thinking "my god, this guy could blow his brains out in the next couple of seconds"'.[9]

Why should the viewer's raptness in the event in this situation be viewed as any different from the experience, say, of reading a book where one may be similarly swept away into a diegesis that imposes its own structures of relevance, its own thematic fields and horizons? In such situations, too, the objects and relations in one's immediate vicinity may become momentarily backgrounded in favour of an intense engagement with an alternate province of reality (Schutz and Luckmann, 1973: 193). As this chapter has demonstrated, the difference can be

---

[8] *Russian Roulette Revisited,* Channel 4, October 2003.

[9] Dominik Diamond (2003), *The Star.* Quoted at http://www.derrenbrown.co.uk/news/roulette (accessed 20 January 2006).

located in the atelicity of the live event. The reader encountering the world of the book is indeed encountering it in the emergent *now* of reading, in an ever-novel *now*-moment. The book's narrative, though, was over and done with before the reader opened the book. No matter how much an author may choose to deny the reader closure, one can always skip to the last page to see how it ends, just as one can fast-forward a DVD or video to get to the final chapter of the film or to the conclusion of an event recorded earlier; or one can read a review which will furnish one with clues as to how the narrative will develop, just as one can watch a film trailer and encounter key elements of the story in advance. Those elements are available to be encountered because the narrative has already been written. The live event, by contrast, is in the process of being written even as one encounters it; it is coming into being in the world *right now*. To be in the presence of the live event is thus to be swept away into a moment which is transpiring simultaneously with the *now* of one's engagement with it; it is to be *in the event* even as the event endures.

Or to be more precise it is to be in the *television* event as it endures. In the aftermath of the *Russian Roulette* programme it became widely known that the broadcast has not been relayed live but had been transmitted with a short time delay in case anything went badly awry with the stunt.[10] Viewers tuning in at the time would have been unlikely to have been aware of this time delay, not least because of the presence, throughout, of the word 'live' chromakeyed on the screen. To watch the programme was thus to believe oneself to be in the presence of an event that was transpiring in the emergent *now* of viewing. This was not the case. As I sat in my living room engrossed in the spectacle of Brown staring palely into space with the gun on the table in front of him, so Brown was *right now*, in the farmhouse on the island of Jersey where he had carried out the stunt, striding across the room to embrace James, the bullet safely fired into the sandbag. Brown and I were in the same emergent *now*, just as we will always and inevitably be for as long as we both endure in the world; but the *now* in which I would watch him finally pick up the gun from the table was not the *now* in which he had done so. The atelic event which was simultaneous with the moment of my encountering it, in other words, was not the event-in-the-world but the television event. The complex relationship between the two will be explored in the next chapter, as we examine in more detail the relationship between liveness and mediation.

---

[10]It also emerged that the gun had been loaded with blanks rather than with live ammunition, although Brown was adamant that a blank would have done a commensurate amount of damage to him at such close range.

5

The Mediation of the Event

5.1 Time, Space and Transformation

From a Bergsonian perspective we might wish to conclude that there are no events in the world but only *flux*, a ceaseless unfolding everywhere of an ever-new now-moment.[1] If our encounters with the world yield to us determinate patterns and orderings, if we interpret and configure certain moments as standing in a particular causal relation to each other, then this is a consequence of our sense-making activities as entities who endure in the universe in the same emergent present as the events which we apprehend around us. The event, from this point of view, is a construct. In the world, simply, stuff happens. It is the observation of this 'stuff' by intentional beings which transmutes it into an event with a more-or-less recognizable beginning, middle and end, a history and a set of possible outcomes. The event, in other words, is a phenomenon that comes into being only through our mediation of the world.

Viewed from the perspective of the broadcast audience, little of this matters. Whether there are events in the world or not is largely immaterial. To view an event is in any case to watch something that has been mediated through the sense-making activities of television. We can never access the world through the broadcast; we can only access the world of the broadcast, a world that has been multiply-mediated on its way from the remote places in which it unfolded to the locale in which we encounter it. The world of the event, as we encounter it when we switch on our televisions, is the world of the television event.

Consider the ways in which the stuff of the world comes to be transformed into the material of the television event. In the next chapter I will be examining in some detail the broadcasting of live election night coverage; for now, we may take a single moment from this kind of television event as a preliminary example. Let's say that in a hall somewhere in the south of England a constituency count has just been concluded and the candidates are lined up on the stage, waiting for the declaring officer to read out the results. A television company has a crew present to capture what can be seen and heard. This is the first moment in the process of transformation through which the stuff of the world comes to be the event that we encounter on television: image and sound are captured on the spot in the real time in which stuff is happening. Into the camera operator's earpiece

---

[1] An earlier draft of some of the material in this chapter originally appeared in Marriott (1996).

comes an instruction from the director in the scanner parked outside the hall to get a tighter shot of one of the candidates, who is expected to lose his parliamentary seat at any moment. The operator reframes the shot. If this one moment comes to be selected for transmission further up the line, it will be this particular framing of the stuff of the world – a medium close-up of the candidate's expression, say, rather than a medium long shot or a long shot in which he is seen in the line-up of candidates as one amongst many – which will come to be constitutive of the event.

There are a number of different destinations through which this first-generation material must pass, and a number of transformations which may happen to it along the way. The scanner will transmit this particular slice of the world to a local hub, where it will manifest itself on a monitor alongside other monitors displaying other slices of the world which are being captured in other constituency counts, constituency associations, local party headquarters and the like. Here a producer may select it, in consultation with some individual or individuals in the control gallery in London, to be relayed onwards as one of a number of candidates for broadcast which are being transmitted to the central hub and then on to the central control gallery, from up and down the country. Let's suppose that the director or editor in this central control gallery deems this moment to be sufficiently significant to become part of the live programme. At this point the moment may undergo any one of a series of further transformations. It will, for one thing, be inserted into the live flow of the broadcast where it will assume a set of syntagmatic relations with the material that has preceded it and the material which comes to follow it. It may, too, appear on the video wall in the election night studio, where it may come to be talked through in the instant of its unfolding by the anchor in the studio; and it will appear on television screens and monitors in local constituency associations and party headquarters, where it may form the backdrop for exultation or despair on the part of individuals who are in turn captured on television watching the moment unfold. All of this, from the framing of the stuff of the world to its live transmission, has occurred in the blink of an eye: instantaneously or near-instantaneously, in the live flow of the broadcast.

Now the moment becomes increasingly plastic, a text which can be worked upon, squeezed, expanded, over-written, re-written. Graphics may appear on the surface of the image, showing the tally of results for one party or another or the number of votes for each candidate, either in this seat or in others. Relayed to another room in the same building it may become part of the videotape operator's box of tricks, to be collated with other images of other moments into a montage which will be played and replayed at intervals during the night. As a consequence it will enter into a different set of syntagmatic relations with a different set of images drawn from a different set of places. There may now be music, as well, accompanying the montage, which serves to remark mischievously on the material on display, with individual images edited into the sequence in such a way that the song in question serves as an informal commentary; or the material may be accompanied, once again, by some kind of a voiceover commentary.

The moment may come to be selected and re-selected in the aftermath of the event too, turning up perhaps in documentary footage where it may serve a variety of functions. Here, however, we will cease to track its progress. The point of the exercise should by now be clear. Television has wrought a series of transformations upon the stuff of the world. In narrative terms, first, it has come to be positioned as part of a sequence or sequences which have construed it in particular ways and endowed it with particular kinds of significance. Second, the place in which this particular stuff happened has been articulated with the other places drawn into the live broadcast: the studio, other constituency counts, the homes of party leaders and so on. In the process, the broadcast has brought about a shift or a number of shifts in the way in which the set of spatial relations between one place and another can be experienced. Finally, it has undergone a series of temporal transformations. At the original moment of transmission, all the stages in the delivery of the moment – stuff happening, its capture, its transmission and its reception in a multiplicity of remote sites – were simultaneous. Processes of recording, of montage and replay mean that there is now a disjuncture between the moment of capture and the moment of transmission, such that the moment is no longer live. It may, too, have become subject to other kinds of temporal transformation such as slow-motion or ellipsis, so that it now occupies a different time interval, longer or shorter, than the original interval in which it unfolded in the world.

5.2   The Multiple Mediations of the Event

This brief discussion of the genesis of the live television event highlights its phenomenal spatial and temporal complexity. In the world, stuff happens in just one place at just one moment, i.e., it happens *here* and *now*. The live television event, too, may deliver to its audience the goings-on in a single place and time if it is constructed around, say, a live concert or studio discussion. Equally, however, it may involve the articulation of a multiplicity of different locales. It may, furthermore, involve a range of different *now*-moments as well, if recorded segments form part of the material of the programme. In the world, then, there is only ever *this* place and *this* time; but the live television event may span a number of different places, some of them simultaneous and some of them not.

In the world, too, stuff comes into being all at once in the emergent present. The material of the live television event, by contrast, emerges from a process of accretion in which a number of rapid-fire decisions shape and select both image and sound and embed them in the flow of the broadcast. These multiple mediations – some of them simultaneous, some of them serial – give rise to an event which is both multi-layered and multi-modal, in which an aggregation of elements from diverse times and places – images, sounds, graphics – enter into the process at different stages of its development.

What kinds of consequences do these two characteristics of the live television event – its delivery of a multiplicity of different places and different moments, and its multiple mediations of the stuff of the world – have for the kinds of forms and structures which arise? In the following chapters I will consider this question in relation to the spatial complexity of the event. In this chapter I will be examining the kinds of temporal transformations that arise as a consequence of the intricate set of relations between the television event and the world.

We may start by noting that there are a number of different moments which are crucial to the construction of the live event. When I watch 'fully' live television, all of these moments are simultaneous: stuff happens, television captures it, television inscribes it in any one of a number of ways, it is transmitted and it turns up for me to view. As soon as the live event comes to incorporate segments that are not fully live, however, then a number of factors may intervene to rupture the simultaneity of some one moment in the construction of the event with some other.

There may, for instance, be a disjuncture between the *now* in which television captures the event and the *now* in which it is transmitted. This is the situation which we encountered in the discussion of *Russian Roulette* at the end of the previous chapter. As I watched, Derren Brown held a gun at arm's length and successfully fired the blank bullet into the sandbags at the other end of the room; but in the real world, he had already slammed the gun back down on the table and was walking away to embrace James, with every appearance of relief on his face. The stunt with the gun and television's capture of the stunt were, as they always must be, simultaneous. Television can only capture the world in the moment of its unfolding: a camera cannot record something that happened five minutes ago, but only what is transpiring *right now*. But there was a disjuncture between the *now* of capturing the event and the *now* of transmission, and as a consequence I was unable to experience the world as it happened.

Other disjunctures come about as a result of the multiple mediations and multi-layerings of the event as it passes through processes of production on its journey from the original locale in which stuff happened to the place in which I encounter it. As a particularly complex example of this phenomenon we can consider the talk that is produced during live action replays.

As we saw in the previous chapter, live commentary typically operates in one of two distinct modes. In a historical mode the commentator reflects back on events which are arranged as a telic series with a beginning and end point, the whole of which is anterior to the moment of speech. This kind of talk indicates a speaker who is not *in medias res*; may well know the outcome; will be apprised of the set of causes and effects which informed what came to transpire; and can discuss the whole from the kind of god's-eye-view which is the consequence of knowing the ins and outs of the event before one begins to speak it.

In an experiential mode, by contrast, we encounter a speaker who is surfing the wave of the *now*. All that transpires is viewed from the perspective of this *now*-moment in which stuff is happening, has just happened or is about to happen. In the examples below, for instance, we can see the way in which commentators move between a current state of affairs ('That is a bad cut'; 'Looks good, looks very good'), an immediately preceding state of affairs ('he missed a great volleying chance there'; 'He forced a high return') and what could happen next ('the referee will have to have a good look at that and the doctors too'; 'Even if he fails with this one he's got another one left to adjust'):

1. That is a bad cut. It's right at the corner and the referee will have to have a good look at that and the doctors too. [boxing]
2. And I think very sensibly drawing for the shot, Jim. Even if he fails with this one he's got another one left to adjust. Looks good, looks very good. [bowls]
3. So he missed a great volleying chance there. He forced a high return. [tennis]

The linguistic system of tense plays a predictable role in this kind of experiential commentary. The present tense, characteristically, is used for the description of what is happening at the moment of utterance, and for the prediction of what may come to pass; and the simple past tense, generally, for the description of what happened immediately before the moment of speech. The use of these tense alternations effectively divides the world of the game into two distinct temporally and causally related zones, whereby the use of the past indicates an earlier state of affairs and the use of the present, a situation which has come about *as a consequence*:

4. That was his second choice, but uh he may have the angle on the green here to continue his break. [snooker]
5. Finished fractionally straight on the blue but not really gonna be any great problem. He can just run through them. His next red is one to the left hand corner pocket. [snooker]

The tense alternations here ('That *was* his second choice, but uh he *may* have an angle on the green'; '*Finished* fractionally straight … but … He *can* just run through them') permit the speakers both to describe a past situation and then to segue seamlessly into a discussion of what might happen as a result. Such alternations are typical of the kind of live talk which we find when a commentator is talking through an event which is happening in the generative *now*, unfolding at the moment of speech.

There is, however, a species of live commentary in which the alternations between past and present do not simply signify a causal chaining of events. In the talk produced during replays, commentators seem equally likely to talk about the action in the past or in the present, and may even appear to alternate randomly between the two:

6. Nice little knock back from Klinsmann. It's well struck by Sammer and the keeper does enough. [football]
7. Wilander hitting the returns with such deadly accuracy. That one just clipped the top of the net. [tennis]
8. Yeah, long passes here. Oldham certainly not afraid to throw the ball wide. Kuiti throws a missed pass onto the wing, Ranson gets low into the corner, yes, just managed to get the ball down there. I think it was a great decision. [rugby]

9.   And it's the Englishman who finally penetrates his armour. He blocks one, he blocks two, but he couldn't block three. [indoor hockey]

10. See, he just plays a little bit wide of the target, doesn't quite get the angle, removes the two at the front, but missed that all important blue shot biting the blue four foot circle. [curling]

11. Well Wilander really had to be cool on this point because it's a good return. McEnroe plays a delicate half volley, but how well Wilander moves to that forehand. [tennis]

In (6), the present tense is used to remark on what is currently happening ('It's well struck'; 'the keeper *does* enough'). In (7), the past tense is used for the same purpose ('That one just *clipped* the top of the net'). In (8)–(11) the speakers alternate between tenses, despite the fact that they are commenting on a chronological series of events: Kuiti *throws a missed pass* and Ranson *gets low in the corner* but then *managed* to get the ball down; the goalkeeper *blocks one* and *blocks two* but *couldn't* block three attempts at the goal; the player *plays* a little wide of the target, *removes* the two at the front but *missed* his next target; Wilander *had to be cool*, McEnroe *plays a delicate half volley* and then Wilander *moves* to the forehand.

At first glance, these apparently unmotivated shifts from a present to a past frame of reference look rather like the kinds of alternations that occur in oral narratives when speakers shift into the historic present:

12. Yesterday, I was quietly sitting in my favourite hang-out and sipping a beer, as I always do at this time of day. All of a sudden, a man to my left turns to me, grins and says: 'Let's get out of here!' (Klein, 1994: 134)

13. Do you know what John did to me the other day? Well, just as I was leaving for the office, he comes in and tells me I've won on the pools and some big chap will come and pay me over £1,000. I nearly fainted on the spot. And two minutes later he tells me it's all a hoax and I haven't won anything at all. (DeClerk, 1991: 72)

Extracts (12) and (13) look very similar in some ways to the previous extracts, with an apparently fluid set of alternations between a past frame of reference ('I *was* quietly sitting'; 'just as I *was* leaving for the office') and the present ('a man to my left *turns* to me'; 'he *comes* in and *tells* me'). There is, however, a significant difference. The shifts into the present tense in (12) and (13) are indicative of narrators who are talking about the past *as if* events were unfolding in the generative *now* of speech; they involve, in other words, a 'shift of temporal perspective' (DeClerk, 1991: 75), a 'metaphorical' realignment of speaker and situation whereby the individual uses the present to talk about a situation which 'really obtains' (Klein, 1994: 138) in the past. The talk produced during replays is fundamentally different from this. During a replay, commentators are able to shift from past to present and back again because they are talking through a set of circumstances in which the situation 'really obtains' in *both* the past and the present, as I will demonstrate in what follows.

5.3   Reprising Reality: The Live Action Replay

From a phenomenological perspective, replays involve an intricate and elaborate re-ordering of the time-space characteristics of the canonical encounter, the world of co-presence in which we experience events as unfolding *here*, *now*, and once and for all (Morris and Nydahl, 1985: 102; Morse, 1983: 49). Consider the situation which holds during a fully live segment of a tennis match. In the world, stuff is happening: players are moving around a court, hitting a ball across a net, scoring points, arguing with the umpire, changing ends. Live television, characteristically, transmutes these occurrences into a real-time linear sequence which is simultaneous with the unfolding of stuff in the world. A player tosses a ball into the air and hits the ball with his racquet; the ball flies across the court to be intercepted by the individual on the other side of the net. Just so in the live broadcast these moments follow one after the other in the generative *now* in which they transpire.

The situation is quite otherwise during a replay. In the world, stuff continues to happen; the players have completed a game, perhaps, and are now sitting at the side of the court before changing ends to continue the match. On television, too, events are unfolding, but they are no longer simultaneous with the stuff of the world. Once again, on the screen, the player at the end of the court nearest the camera serves to his opponent; once again his opponent attempts to return the serve. Now the image changes and a further sequence is displayed on the screen, which exhibits once again a disjuncture with the time in which stuff is happening in the world: the conclusion of the rally, which was initiated by the serve reprised at the beginning of the replay. Finally there is a cut to the players walking back out on to the court to continue the match, and we are back in real time.

At first glance this sequence of events may appear to be little different, phenomenologically, from the time-delayed *Russian Roulette* broadcast. In both instances, television has captured the stuff of the world in real time; in both, there is a delay between capture and transmission, with the consequence that the audience is unable to encounter the event in the generative *now* in which it is unfolding. Both the *Russian Roulette* broadcast and the live action replay, in other words, involve *asynchrony*: a mismatch between the 'time of the telling' and the 'time of the thing told' (Metz, 1974: 18).

There are good reasons, however, to suppose that the phenomenology of the live action replay is considerably more complex than this. The replay, first of all, characteristically involves a slow-motion dilation of the time of the event, an expansion and stretching of the interval in which stuff originally transpired. Second, replays involve what Genette (1980: 35) has described as *anachronies* or temporal re-orderings. The stuff of the world, as we have seen, is chronologically ordered: a tennis player hits a ball, say, which is returned by his opponent, giving rise to a rally which culminates in the winning of a game and a change of ends. In the course of its transmutation into the material of the replay, however, this sequence comes to be re-written, producing a different syntagmatic relationship between its constitutive elements.

Some sequences, still, are sequentially ordered – we see the player once again miss the final shot in the rally and begin to walk towards the side of the court – but the next elements in the sequence may be the beginning of the rally again, followed perhaps by a shot of the players returning to the court for the next game as we return to real time. The replay, then, characteristically appears to exhibit a fracturing of the Newtonian chronology which governs the unfolding of stuff in the world.

In the course of these transformations, too, the replay gives rise to an intricate set of re-embeddings in which elements of the world come to be iteratively re-told. During the replay the television image is made up of material which has already been seen on the screen, in a different temporal and spatial form. The broadcast thus comes to be composed, momentarily, of an earlier segment of itself, which is occurring for a second time, or possibly for a third or a fourth time, if consecutive sequences are broadcast which show the same phenomenon from different points of view. At such moments the television event, comes to resemble nothing so much as a *kleinform* (Ryan, 1974, cited in Ong, 1977: 320), a 'tube containing part of itself' which 'can in turn be contained in another part of itself, or can emerge from itself and re-enter'.

These iterative re-rackings of the material of the television event have an extraordinary phenomenological consequence. Experientially, the images which constitute the replay have a dual temporal status, existing in both the past and the present at one and the same time. As the sequence unfolds on the television screen it forms a seamless whole: the players sit on their chairs at the side of the court; they take part in a particular rally; they sit on their chairs again, and then stroll back on to the court. One image succeeds another on the screen, each one manifesting itself in the *now* of transmission and reception. From this point of view the sequence which constitutes the replay is happening *now*, in the emergent present in which all stuff transpires in the world. However, the images which are unfolding on the screen – the player hitting a ball, running across the court to anticipate the return and so on – are images of a situation which 'really happened' earlier, and which appeared in real time on-screen at that point as part of the television event. From this second point of view, the replay sequence took place *then*, not *now*. Viewed as part of the syntagmatic chain which is unfolding on the screen, then, the replay is happening *now*; but viewed as anachrony – as a series of elements which have been narratively reconstructed in the present moment of the television event – the replay is clearly *then*.

A further layer of complexity is added by the relationship between these reiterated images of the event and the sound which accompanies them. The *Russian Roulette* broadcast, once we come to know of the time delay, possesses an unequivocal temporal status: it is not live. The material which is transmitted during an action replay, by contrast, is composed of both live and non-live elements. During the replay, the outside broadcast microphones continue to pick up ambient sound; the commentators continue to produce commentary; and commentary and ambient sound are mixed in the real time of transmission and reception. This mix of real-time sound and live commentary continues to be broadcast live during the replay. The sequence of images which constitute the replay, however, are not live. Replay technology, as I have said, creates the conditions for the recapitulation of stuff which 'really happened' some moments or minutes before, dislocated from its 'real' location in time and re-manifesting itself in the emergent *now* of the television event. The material which is transmitted during a replay is thus a fusion of the live, in the form of commentary and ambient sound, and the non-live, in the form of anachronistic and asynchronic images.

It is just precisely these characteristics of the action replay which give rise to the apparently random alternations between simple past and present tenses which occur during commentary. Live commentary is premised upon a real-time talking-through of the material which is transpiring at the generative *now* of speech; but in the case of replays, this material is both past and present, both *then* (a telic sequence whose parameters have already been witnessed and interpreted as they originally manifested themselves some moments ago) and *now* (as it iteratively and anachronistically reappears on the screen).

A brief consideration of this phenomenon from the point of view of the commentator should make clear the extraordinary dual status of the image in such cases. In the utterance below, produced during a change of ends in a tennis match, the commentator begins with a series of remarks which talk through what has just happened, then shifts to talk about the replay which is currently unfolding on the screen, returning to a more generally evaluative mode after the replay has finished:

14. Well there are signs now that uh John McEnroe really has got his eye in well and truly. And uh a couple of things happening in that last game. I thought there that uh the serve is getting very much more bite, particularly to the advantage side, and that is the the slice serve which goes wide to uh the backhand of Mats Wilander is the one which of course favours a left hander terrifically on a fast court like a grass court. And he takes Wilander out wide, and that was a serve I think that uh was an advantage for him against his many matches with Borg on this court. AND THE SAME SITUATION OCCURS HERE. HE REALLY LEAPS INTO THAT BALL WITH A LOT OF BODY ROTATION AND VERY QUICKLY INTO THE NET AND PUNCHING THE FOREHAND AWAY. NOW THIS IS THE OVERHEAD, A DIFFICULT ONE. HE'S FAIRLY DEEP IN THE COURT BUT HE HIT THAT SO HARD THAT MATS WILANDER STRUGGLED TO CONTROL THE RACKET ON THE FOREHAND SIDE. So there are two things happening here, (a) McEnroe is actually utilizing his serve much better, but (b) he's now starting to get weight of shot. And Wilander struggling to control that weight of shot. [tennis]

Extract (14) contains a mixture of tenses. During the first part of the utterance, the commentator produces a series of remarks in the present tense ('John McEnroe really has got his eye in'; 'the serve is getting very much more bite') before going on to make a statement about the player's form ('that was a serve … that uh was an advantage for him against his many matches with Borg on this court'). The replay talk is different, containing an apparently random shift from a present frame of reference ('he really leaps into that ball'; 'this is the overhead') to a past frame of reference ('he hit that so hard'; 'Mats Wilander struggled') as the replay unfolds on screen. Finally there is a shift back to evaluative comments in the present tense ('McEnroe is actually utilizing his serve much better'; 'he's now starting to get weight of shot').

This shift from one mode of description to another parallels a shift in the temporal status of the television event. In the first part of (14), the images on screen are simultaneous with the stuff that is transpiring in the world: as the players drape towels around their necks and take a drink in 'real' time, so the image of these actions appears on the screen. In the middle passage, however, the relationship between the television event and the world of stuff has shifted. In the world, the break between games continues; but on the screen, time-dilated images of an earlier situation are now unfolding. It is just at this point that the commentator produces the alternations between past and present tenses to describe the action as he currently experiences it. These alternations precisely reflect the indeterminate temporal status of the material. Viewed as anachrony – as an earlier segment reiterated in the emergent *now* of commentary – it is clearly 'then'; but viewed as part of the syntagmatic chain which is unfolding before the commentator's eyes as he speaks, it is happening 'now'. The use of the simple past here (*hit, struggled*) mirrors the status of the replay sequence as 'then'; the use of the present tense (*leaps, is*), its status as 'now'. The talk produced during replays, in other words, shifts between a historical and an experiential mode of description as the commentator talks his way through material which exists for him both in the past and in the present at one and the same time.

5.4   Time, Tense and Disjunctures

We should now be in a position to make good on the claim that the alternations between past and present forms in replay commentary are different from the use of the historic present in oral narratives. As I argued earlier in this chapter, the historic present ('just as I was leaving for the office, he *comes* in and tells me …') manifests itself as a consequence of a speaker acting *as if* some past situation were transpiring in the emergent *now* of the narrative. The alternations between historical and experiential modes of description during replays, on the other hand, involve the narration of an event sequence which 'really obtains' both in the past (when it originally appeared on the screen) and in the present (when it is reprised). The historic present, in other words, involves a representation of a past event which is constructed solely through the agency of the speaker. The speaker represents the event as something which is occurring in the emergent *now* of speech, but this representation has no material foundation in the world: it is not available perceptually for either speaker or hearer to observe in the real time of narration. The focus of replay talk, by contrast, is a real-time temporal sequence which manifests itself quite separately from the speaker and which has an independent existence in time and space.

There is, however, one important similarity between the use of the historic present in oral narratives and the alternations between historical and experiential modes of description in replay commentary. Both have to do with the attitude or perspective which the speaker adopts towards the events under discussion. The use of the historical present is not random; rather, it marks the attitude of a speaker who is momentarily choosing to treat some slice of the past as if it were transpiring at the *now* of speech. The shifts in replay talk from current to non-current frames of reference, similarly, are not entirely arbitrary. The transition from one tense to another, when it occurs, is motivated by a systematic choice of one point of view over another. When commentators are focusing on what is happening *now* on the screen, a present tense is selected; where they are concentrating rather on the events *as they originally viewed them* then they will use the past. These systematic and motivated transitions between one temporal perspective and the other can be seen in extracts (15) and (16), taken from the commentary produced during a horse-racing replay:

15.   I just wonder looking at that as we watch him in action really cantering, he's off the bridle now but he just uh allowed Bocaro to really fight, he took his last two hurdles really well. When we saw some of those wonderful shots down the back he didn't really jump so well as I said, but when he needs to he really does uh fly them, and that really has sealed the uh race for uh Graham Bradley. Watch him change his hand there, get a nice hold of the uh rein, just had a look round see what he's gonna do, waving his stick at him, just giving him a crack there to keep him up to his uh work and you can see it's really made him really stretch, get his head down and his belly close to the ground and he's really galloping to the line …

16.   A   Here's this these lovely shots and uh look at him come up long there. I think this is although this is only a little horse he could go and jump fences one day. Watch Brad, look at him just chasing the horse away then grabbing hold of him, and he's got a nice short hold of his uh reins. 's it's a that was a lovely lovely shot in getting a horse away from a hurdle and balanced before you pick him up. And he's really running now …

     B   Yes, what was a a good uh shot also is that Brad is gritting his teeth and I should think shouting at Bocaro to go, 'cause the voice does actually motivate them, and Brad's teeth are gritted, he knows he's got it but look at his grimace on his face. Now I think that tells it all, doesn't it, the grimace from uh pain goes to joy …

Extract (15) opens with an explicit reference to the action currently unfolding in the replay ('looking at that as we watch him in action'), and continues in the present tense ('he's off the bridle now') as the speaker talks through the action in the emergent *now* of live commentary. The shift to a historical mode of description in the next section of the utterance ('he took his last two hurdles really well') is followed by an equally explicit reference to an earlier time frame ('When we saw some of those wonderful shots down the back'), the speaker continuing within this frame as he describes what he has already seen once ('he didn't really jump so well') which he discussed at the time ('as I said'). A remark in the timeless present about the horse's form ('when he needs to he really does uh fly them') is followed by a further transition into an experiential mode, accompanied by an exhortation to the listener to look at what is happening in the intersubjective *now* of production, transmission and reception ('Watch him'), together with an explicit recognition of the shared nature of the live experience ('and you can see'). The speaker continues from this point of view, describing what is occurring at the generative *now* of speech ('it's really made him really stretch, get his head down and his belly close to the ground and he's really galloping to the line').

Similar mechanisms inform the commentary in (16). The first speaker explicitly signals the beginning of a reprise ('Here's this these lovely shots') and again directly addresses the temporally co-present audience ('look at him'; 'Watch Brad, look at him') before expressing an appreciation of the excellence of the original camera work via a transition to a historical mode ('that was a lovely lovely shot'). The second commentator takes up this theme in turn, praising the original camera work before going on to consider the image as it is now available in the present ('what *was* a a good uh shot also is that Brad *is* gritting his teeth') and again exhorting the audience to gaze at the image as it is reiterated on the screen ('look at his grimace on his face').

The same kind of systematic alternations occur elsewhere. Commentators, for example, can be seen to produce overt references to their reactions to the event when they originally saw it, the first time around:

17.   More than anything it was the speed at which he got over his hurdles *that impressed me* on this ground. [horse racing]
18.   He shortened that [—],[2] that was a left and a right, and Branco at that stage looked for all the world like he would go. It was a great piece of uh combination punching by the big commonwealth champion from Telford, Richie Woodhall. *Really we thought he was gone.* [boxing]

References to the re-racked event as it is currently unfolding on the screen, by contrast, are frequently accompanied by exhortations to the audience to look at what is happening, as in (19) and (20) ('Look how early McEnroe is'; 'look at that low backhand drive volley'); by comments which acknowledge the audience's presence in the shared emergent *now* of viewing, as in (20) and (21) ('a shot that you'll see coming up in a minute'; 'as you see here'); or by appeals to the action currently unfolding on the screen as a token of veridicality ('It's obvious right there', in (22)):

19.   Well the serve into the backhand. Look how early McEnroe is when he takes that ball but his return was not deep enough 'cause it gave too much scope for Wilander to play the backhand. [tennis]
20.   Few players in this championship can play a shot that you'll see coming up in a minute. There's the forehand drive, and it's returned well but look at that low backhand drive volley from about a foot off the ground. The odds against making that are tremendous. [tennis]

---

[2] Indicates indecipherable material.

21. He's moving around in the air, as you see here. He doesn't drop it, keeps hold of it. [football]
22. And Edgar Bennett, there he goes he grabs the face mask. It's obvious right there he did grab the face mask himself. [American football]

Such invocations of one or the other temporal perspective are marked above all else by the presence or absence of direct address. Direct address, though common in sports announcing (Whannel, 1992: 108), occurs relatively infrequently in live commentary, which mostly eschews interactivity in favour of a monological address to the audience. Direct address during replays, when it does occur, typically functions to draw the audience's attention to some aspect of the current action, as in extracts (19) to (21), and is thus associated with a present frame of reference.

5.5 Television Eats Itself: Re-racking the Event

The presence of direct address in the above extracts does not only help to identify the use of an experiential mode of description; it will also serve to alert us to a further complexity in the material. The choice of a historical or experiential mode in replay talk would appear, at first glance, to be dependent upon the commentators' perspectives on events as they are currently unfolding in the generative *now* of speech. Commentators are, after all, generally "'live", i.e., on the spot, and simultaneous to the "crowd" event' (Morse, 1983: 53), and are therefore in a position to directly witness and thus remark upon what is transpiring before their eyes from their vantage point in the commentary box. A brief glance back over the extracts we have been considering will make it entirely clear, however, that live commentary characteristically takes as its point of departure not the speakers' own unmediated view of the scene but rather the mediation of the event as it is unfolding on the monitor or television screen in their vicinity. That this is transparently the case can be demonstrated, first of all, by the kinds of expressions which directly index some element of the television event for the edification of the viewer. When commentators exhort the audience to 'look at that low backhand drive volley' or to 'look at how early McEnroe is when he takes that ball', they are able to do so only by virtue of being able to presuppose a shared perceptual field which is jointly available to anyone who is attending to the screen. The other examples we have already examined in extracts (19)–(22) function in a similar manner.

There is, furthermore, an even more compelling piece of evidence that the talk produced during replays is largely based on the television event rather than on the speaker's unmediated encounter with the stuff of the world. In the world, stuff happens once and once only. If the material of the replay has a dual temporal status as both *then* and *now*, then it possesses this status only by virtue of its re-enactment on the screen. The world that speakers index as *now* during replay commentary can only be the world of the television event.

This is not to argue that commentators never base their remarks under any circumstances on their own unmediated view of the world around them.

On occasions, clearly, commentators do refer to what is directly passing before their eyes. In (23) and (24) below, for instance, we can see examples of speakers adding information based on their own view from the commentary box:

23.   Well you didn't see the look on Jimmy's face but I did. And that means he can't get past the other red. [snooker]
24.   Well I'm right in line with the shot Jack, and I don't think he can do it. [snooker]

In both of these cases, however, the speakers explicitly indicate that they are departing from the default point of view ('you didn't see the look ... but I did'; 'I'm right in line with the shot') in order to apprise the audience of information which is only available to someone with unmediated access to the event (the expression on a player's face, off camera; a particular angle on an upcoming snooker shot). The same holds true when significant incidents occur during a replay, and are therefore again unavailable to a remote audience whose only visual access to the event is through the mediation of the screen. Extracts (25) and (26) will serve as examples here:

25.   Well this is a stunning get by McEnroe. He does so well to get his racket on the ball but how quickly Wilander sprinted up to that. *And while all that was going on, McEn uh uh Wilander came to the umpire and asked if he could have the net cord judge move his jacket from the chair. Just in their sort of peripheral vision. These players catch anything that's moving.* [tennis]
26.   Here's a replay. Now you see Fitipaldi go out of the picture there and spinning – *OH! And that's Gerhard Berger.* Well this this this is in effect a replay of Grand Prix that we have seen in these conditions before and I don't know what the answer is but it it proves to me that that it's a farcical situation. [motor racing]

In (25), the commentator updates the audience on something that has occurred in real time during a replay. The same phenomenon occurs in (26), as the speaker airs his excitement at a crash which has occurred in real time on the track whilst a replay of another crash is in progress on screen. The excited *OH!* as he witnesses the second crash is produced some moments before the replay of the first crash is curtailed to make way for real-time coverage of the second one.

What examples (23)–(26) have in common is that they permit commentators to provide supplementary information to the audience on something which is happening out of their sight (as in (23)) or to produce an evaluative judgement based on a momentarily superior vantage point (24) or to fill viewers in on what has just happened in the world whilst the television event was taken up with the work of reiteration. Such moments apart, commentary is typically based not on the world of stuff but on the television event (Marriott, 1995). Characteristically, commentators restrict themselves to talking through what is visibly shared with the audience at home; and they are generally responsive to whatever images turn up on the screen. If a player is shown in close-up, the commentators may choose that moment to remark on some aspect of that player's performance or history; if graphics appear on the screen, the commentators may remark on the information thus displayed, as in (27); and if an incident is shown from a particular angle then they may explicitly discuss it from that point of view, as in (28):

27. 49 points in front, *there you see it*, 59 on the table. [snooker]
28. My word, *this uh camera angle* showing us the intended red that Steve's trying for, but this is really tight into the pocket. [snooker]

Live commentary, then, is restricted by and large to the television event as it manifests itself on the screen. A brief consideration of the difference between radio and television commentary should make it clear why this is the case. Radio commentary is produced for the benefit of an audience which has no visual access to the unfolding event, and which is therefore dependent on talk – together with whatever subset of ambient sound has been selected for transmission – for the mediation and realization of what is happening in the world. Live television commentary, by contrast, serves to accompany an existing set of mediations of the event (in the form of images, sounds and graphics) with which it unfolds in tandem. Its principal function is therefore – occasional interjections and digressions apart – to contextualize and specify this material for the absent audience. But this in turn has an extraordinary phenomenological consequence. Commentary does not simply form one strand in television's narration of the event; it is produced on the basis of a simultaneous viewing of and exposition upon the material of the television event in the real time of production, transmission and reception. Commentary, in short, serves to mediate television's mediation of the stuff of the world, thereby endowing the television event with a complex and self-referential structure whereby one element in the live broadcast continually feeds upon another in the live flow of the broadcast.

That this phenomenal complexity at the heart of the live television event is revealed by a consideration of the talk produced during replays is not surprising. During fully live broadcast segments, the stuff of the world and the material of the television event unfold simultaneously. Something happens; commentary remarks upon what is happening; television offers both of these to the audience in real time; and the elaborate set of relationships between these different moments in the construction of the event do not offer themselves to us as particularly remarkable. It is only during moments of disjuncture such as the replay that we can begin to tease apart the different aspects of the live event and consider the intricate relationships between them. Through replay technology, television constructs a radically different kind of narrative: both live and non-live, present and past, referential and self-referential, consuming itself in a potentially endless cycle of iteration. That this is only one of the complexities which are attendant upon the real-time mediation of the stuff of the world will become clear in the next chapter, where we return to a consideration of space.

6

Space and the Live Event

6.1 Reflections on the Problem of Liveness

Having decided to jot down some thoughts on the matter of liveness, I have
switched on my computer in my office at home. My immediate vicinity is
considerably different from Schutz's in his garden. He has a sheet of paper
in his visual field; I have a screen. In front of him is his table, with his pencil,
two books and other unspecified objects; I am at a desk, cluttered with books
and papers, a telephone, computer peripherals and a number of remote controls.
Beyond Schutz's immediate reach are trees, a lawn, a lake with boats, a mountain,
clouds; beyond mine are two small televisions, a VCR, a DVD recorder and a
pile of DVDs. If he turns his head, Schutz can see his house and the windows
of his room; I see the trees and the grass in the park outside my window and the
cars parked across the road. Schutz hears the buzzing of a motorboat, children's
voices, bird song; I can hear the humming of my hard disk, the distant motorway,
a passing car, my hands on the keyboard.

Schutz is outside, I am inside. But that is the least of the differences between
us. Schutz is engaged in 'a quite specific task' as he sits in his garden: 'the
analysis of the problem of relevance' (Schutz, 1970: 2). To this task, he can
bring the entire contents of his mind: his 'autobiographical situation' and all the
experiences of the world which he has in his memory or his 'stock of knowledge
at hand' in the form of everything he has read or discussed or thought about
which is germane to his current enquiry (Schutz, 1970: 2). I am also engaged in
a specific task: thinking about liveness. The immediate resources at my disposal,
however, seem near-infinite. With one keystroke I can access the internet with
its vast networks of information and opinion. If I enter the words 'Schutz' and
'relevance' into a search engine it comes up, in less than half a second, with over
32,000 pages of results in English alone; if I simply enter 'Schutz' it offers me
some 567,000 pages to view. Entering 'Alfred Schutz' and 'photo' takes me to a
page where the man himself is pictured with a lawn and trees in the background.
He is gazing at the camera, and so appears to be looking at me from his garden
with an inscrutable smile on his face.

Nor is a search engine the only tool at my disposal. Without getting up from
my desk or allowing my eyes to stray from what is immediately in front of me,
I can email a number of colleagues to seek clarification on a particular problem
or to ask for a reference; I can access the online catalogues of university libraries
to check which of them have copies of a particular book or paper which Schutz
has mentioned in what I have just read; I can open an instant messenger program

with a view to interacting with any of my family and friends who are currently online and who may be able to cast light on some particular question. Unlike Schutz's situation in his garden, furthermore, the possibilities for distraction seem endless. I can take a break to check on the progress of a particular item I want to buy at an online auction or to access my bank or credit card account online to see if I can afford it; I can check the weather to see if I will be able to sit in my own garden this afternoon; I can access a news site to see what is going on in the world, either by reading the copy and looking at whatever images are available or by watching recorded clips. Software on my computer, moreover, will permit me to listen to a radio station with my choice of music or news while I sit here typing, or to watch live video. Now the boundaries of what I can hear and see in my immediate vicinity have decisively shifted. I can hear not only my hands striking the computer keyboard, but the voices of individuals delivering speeches at a ceremonial event on the other side of the world and the intermittent sound of applause, brought to me via streaming video on a news site. By the simple actions of turning my head, picking up the television remote and switching on the television across the room, furthermore, I can cause further slices of the world to come rushing into my vicinity.

There is, as well, another important distinction between Schutz's situation and my own. Should Schutz choose to get up from his chair, walk through the house and out into the streets, then he will open up the possibility of encountering an infinite variety of perceptual objects: cars, street signs, houses, trees, other pedestrians, other gardens. The limits of what he can encounter, however, will be circumscribed by the limits of his perceptual boundaries: all he will be able to see and to hear will be those phenomena which fall directly within his immediate vicinity. My situation is different. By carrying with me any one of a number of personal media – a mobile phone, a PDA, a laptop – I can continue, as I move, to access the apparent infinitude of simultaneous elsewheres which are wired for instantaneous connectivity. I can, as well, communicate with those elsewheres by making a phone call or sending a message. Unlike Schutz, for me the world can always be present and interactively available wherever I go, with a range of communicative circuits potentially at hand.

Nowhere are these communicative circuits more interestingly dense than in television. Radio, certainly, can construct multiple relays, either in the space of the studio or between studio and distant location: a panel game featuring rapid interchanges between a number of guests, a phone-in slot where the host can interact, from moment to moment, with different members of the remote audience, a real-time chat between a politician in one studio and a presenter in another. The visual dimension to television, however, makes possible an extraordinary complexity of interactive circuits, held together and rendered transparent by the gaze both of the camera and of individual participants. The host of an audience participation programme asks a question of one of his guests; the guest turns to the host to reply, receives a riposte from a fellow-guest and turns towards her to engage in a momentary altercation. The programme cuts between the host, the first guest and the second guest, then cuts away for a reaction shot from the studio audience, then back to the host and the guests. For a member of the audience watching the programme at home as an 'overhearer' of these exchanges (Heritage, 1985: 99; Heritage and Greatbatch, 1991: 96; Scannell, 1991: 2), the lines of communication seem reasonably clear: the camera zooms in to identify the participants in the altercation, zooms out again and pans to reveal the host on the sidelines; the identity of a member of the studio audience, shouting a comment, is rapidly established via a cut to a different camera. When the individual at home in turn becomes the object of address, this communicative shift is made manifest by the direct gaze of the host to camera and a direct address to the remote audience. The host delivers a familiar homily to the viewer, pointing up the moral of the particular set of discourses that the programme has brought into circulation. Having concluded, he turns away, back to the guests and the studio audience as the production credits roll; teleliterate viewers understand that they are no longer the direct object of address and segue seamlessly back into the role of overhearers, or get up to make themselves a cup of tea.

Flawless at its best, television's mastery of the complex communicative circuits it sets in motion is by no means limited to the construction of interchanges between individuals in the studio, or between presenters in the studio and the audience at home. The latter circuit would seem to be primary: the arc of communication which television establishes between the place of production and the place of reception is what television *is for*, inasmuch as the representations that it produces are explicitly designed to be seen and heard by a distant audience. The material which television relays across space to its remote viewers, however, is by no means made up simply of local encounters between co-present participants. When I switch on my television, the world comes rushing into my vicinity; and innumerable elsewheres may be available for me to encounter.

Some of these elsewheres are simultaneous with my encounter with them: a breakfast show in which two presenters are exchanging playful remarks with each other on a sofa; a home shopping channel in which two men are demonstrating a particular printer; a mystifying segment on the channel L!VE TV in which a man in a medieval archer's costume is interacting with individuals dressed as stock Mexicans. Others unfolded a little while ago, but are accompanied nevertheless by the legend *live* chromakeyed on the screen, such as the images of people sleeping in the *Big Brother* house, transmitted with a time delay in case anything untoward should be transpiring which the channel might not wish to broadcast. Yet others, of course, represent the world as it was hours or days or months or years ago, captured at some other *now*-moment to be transmitted and received in my own.

There are, too, variations in the spatial complexity of the material that is on hand for me to view. Watching *Big Brother Live* at this time of the morning, all I will see is a sequence of images of sleeping individuals, all of them co-present in the same bedroom. The programme will cut from time to time from one bed to another, from a close-up of one man fast asleep to a medium shot of two beds in one of which an individual is flinging out a hand in their sleep as I watch; but all of the relevant cameras are operating within the same locale, and television need therefore do nothing more than to choose which view of the room to broadcast at which moment. Several distinct locales are implicated in my encounter with the sleeping residents of the *Big Brother* house: the bedroom itself; the control gallery, in which some individual or individuals are deciding *right now* which camera to select; my own immediate vicinity in which I am remotely viewing the event. The event itself, however, at the moment of watching, is emanating from a single discrete place. The same is true, *mutatis mutandis*, of the home shopping channel and the L!VE TV segment.

In other control galleries other individuals have a greater degree of spatial diffusion to work with. The breakfast show cuts from the people on the sofa to a weather presenter on a roof overlooking a cloudy London. Now there are four kinds of remote locale involved in the broadcast: the studio, the outside location, the control gallery and the place(s) where I – and others – are watching. The programme cuts back to the studio, then cuts again to a recorded segment within which a number of different sites are brought together within a brief narrative. For the control gallery, this involves a single operation only; but the spatial complexity of the programme has increased once more, with several further locales drawn into the flow of the broadcast and several more slices of the world tumbling, one after another, into my immediate vicinity. For every new locale introduced into the broadcast, furthermore, the spatial intricacy of the material on my screen will increase. The following examination of election night coverage on British television will demonstrate just how complex it can become.[1]

6.2   The Mediation of the Event: Election Night

Be not afeard. The isle is full of noises.

(Shakespeare, *The Tempest*)

It is early morning on 2 May 1997. On BBC1, the British election night results are in full swing. A large number of different locales are implicated in the broadcast. There are the places in which individual members of the audience – a subset of the 6.5 million who have tuned in over the course of the evening[2] – are watching the programme; there is the studio in London from which the presenter, David Dimbleby, is anchoring the results, and the studios in other parts of the country with which Dimbleby occasionally interacts in order to catch up on local results or to interview politicians who are in the area by virtue of the location of their constituencies. There are the constituency counts, in some of which results have already been declared by this point in the broadcast and in others of which counting is still going on or declarations are on the point of being made. There are the national party headquarters, and the local headquarters and clubs. There are the venues in which celebrations are waiting to commence once it becomes clear which side is victorious. There are cars, trains, planes and other forms of transportation in which government ministers, newly elected Members

---

[1] For an earlier draft of this discussion of election night, see Marriott (2000).

[2] http://216.239.59.104/search?q=cache:0lDoVS-CcVAJ:www.ofcom.org.uk/static/archive/itc/uploads/Election_2001_Viewers_Response_to_the_Television_Coverage.pdf+%22election+night%22+1997+AUDIENCE+6.5&hl=en&lr=lang_en (accessed 10 July 2002).

of Parliament, advisors and others are travelling, many of them heading in the direction of London in the aftermath of constituency declarations but some, newly unemployed, heading home.

These places are all remote from one another. They have two elements in common. First, they have been selected by the BBC (and, in some cases, by institutions of the state and/or the political parties as well) as significant nodes in a network whose domain is the election of a new British government. Second, events in these locales are all transpiring simultaneously: they are all occurring *right now*.

A further series of events is happening *right now* too. In most of these remote places, and in some others besides, the machinery of the broadcast is in motion. At some counts, camera crews are still set up in anticipation of a declaration; in others, a victorious or defeated candidate waits in front of a camera to be interviewed by a correspondent or to engage in a down-the-line interview with Dimbleby in London, whilst in yet others a camera operator is following an individual waiting to hear the results or has their camera trained upon the piles of ballot papers being counted in a hall. There are crews at party headquarters and at the Royal Festival Hall in London where the Labour victory celebrations are waiting to begin, and there are crews, presenters, analysts, IT staff and guests in the election night studio in London and in regional studios around the country. There are, too, individuals caught up in the complex chain of command and communication by virtue of which what is transpiring locally is fed into the live broadcast: Outside Broadcast directors and producers in scanners at constituency counts, and at other locales deemed sufficiently important by the broadcast to merit their presence; teams in control galleries in regional studios, some of which are transmitting their own programmes live on the night as well as offering material to BBC1; producers in the seven separate galleries or 'hubs' in which live feeds from around the country are selected to be routed to the control gallery in London; the programme director, the editor, the sound supervisor, the vision mixer and others in the control gallery at BBC Television Centre who are engaging with, selecting and mixing all of these different inputs to produce the live stuff of the broadcast itself.

In the real time of this broadcast, the air is criss-crossed by messages emanating from one remote locale and terminating in some other. In the gallery, an individual is directing instructions to a videotape operator elsewhere in the building with regard to non-simultaneous material which may momentarily be selected for transmission in the *now* of the programme: a montage of footage captured earlier of the Prime Minister arriving at his own constituency count, perhaps, or the leader of the opposition casting his vote earlier in the day, or the first declaration of the night. Another member of the team may be communicating with an OB director or a camera operator in a constituency which is about to announce its results, asking for a tighter shot on a government minister in the line-up who is rumoured to be about to lose her seat. Yet another may be talking to Dimbleby in the studio via the latter's earpiece, alerting him to the sequence which is about to be broadcast: a down-the-line interview with a newly elected MP, and then a cut to a correspondent on a balcony overlooking the crowd in the Royal Festival Hall and on to the Tory Party Chairman at Conservative Central Office in Smith Square in London. Dimbleby, in the election night studio, completes an interchange with his colleague Jeremy Paxman who is hosting a round-table discussion in one part of the studio, turns to camera to address the audience at home for a moment then turns away towards the video wall to chat with the remote individual who the control gallery has informed him will be next up in the morning's interviews. In the hubs and in the outside broadcast locations, meanwhile, crews are interacting with each other to capture particular elements of particular scenes on camera and to choose particular shots to offer for transmission. Beyond the reach or the direct intervention of television, furthermore, other individuals are engaging in remote encounters as well. MPs are being paged by their party. Mobile phones are ringing as government advisors are alerted to another expected or unexpected loss of a seat, or as a member of the incoming government, in a plane en route to London, is briefed by a secretary as to the reception that awaits him on his arrival.

Many individuals, too, are watching television. Some are members of the audience at home, with no relation to the events going on around the country other than that of members of the electorate who feel sufficiently interested in the outcome to be still up and watching at this hour. Others are more central actors in the night's events. Over the course of the evening, in different places and at different times, many of these have tuned in to the BBC or to the other channels broadcasting the results. In Hartlepool, the Labour campaign manager Peter Mandelson watches television in his own count as the Conservatives lose their first seat of the evening in Birmingham, refusing to let the cameras film him as he waits for the result; after his own declaration at Sedgefield, Tony Blair goes upstairs to watch the results on television before heading off to London by plane; at his house in Huntingdon, the Conservative leader John Major watches television in his dressing gown, groaning when he hears 'a particularly unexpected loss or a loss of someone that he counted as a friend'; at Conservative Central Office, aides in the war room watch as the television results panel turns into a 'sea of red'; in a car in London, Major's press secretary watches television and listens to the radio as the Blairs arrive at their victory party, hoping that the Majors, in the car behind, don't have their radio on.[3]

This ubiquity of sets and screens leads to a complex interpenetration of conditions of production and reception. In the control gallery, a bank of monitors displays images from around the country, including the shot currently selected for transmission. If the team in the gallery is thus simultaneously cast in the role of consumers of the text and participants in its construction then they are by no means alone. BBC1's coverage of the night's events features numerous images of individuals caught in the act of viewing television. Alex Salmond, leader of the Scottish National Party, is seen at his count at Banff and Buchan, looking jubilantly at the television as the SNP gain the seat of Galloway in Scotland; and individuals – Blair's supporters in Sedgefield, for example – are also caught on

---

[3] Incidents drawn from *A Night to Remember*, Channel 4, 18 April 1998.

camera in moments of endless regress, watching themselves watching themselves on a large screen in an example of what Ong (1977: 318), in a related context, refers to as a 'one-way electronic hall of mirrors'.

Throughout, it is the studio, perpetually at the centre, which forms the matrix in which this unfolding and multiply-mediated event is embedded. The set itself supplies a clue as to the programme makers' intentions here, designed to 'create the impression of a hub, with spokes radiating outwards to every corner of the country'.[4] Dimbleby sits at a large circular table in the centre, accompanied by a number of political commentators and psephologists, with two large screens in the background, a graphics screen and a video wall displaying feeds from remote locations. Throughout the programme, interactions with these locations are mediated in a way that makes it entirely evident that the studio is the 'institutional discursive space' (Scannell, 1991: 2) from which the broadcast speaks. In one characteristic sequence early on in the programme, Dimbleby talks in turn to correspondents at three remote sites. The sequence opens with a shot of all three locales simultaneously but separately framed on the main screen of the video wall. Two of the windows subsequently slide away to be replaced by a full-size shot of the first reporter, Jeremy Vine at Labour Party headquarters, seen first on the screen with Dimbleby seated in the studio foreground and then in an 'unmediated' shot, speaking directly to camera. At the end of this first interview the broadcast returns to frame again all three sites on the studio screen before parallel cuts to the second and then the third interview. The sequence ends with a final shot of the third correspondent, seen on the studio screen being addressed by a foregrounded Dimbleby. This sequence is typical of the way in which the relationship between studio and remote locations is handled. Reporters and interviewees are invariably seen first on the studio screen before the programme cuts to a full shot of the remote location, and participants at remote sites on no occasion directly address each other, commenting always through the mediation of the studio, and of the anchor, at the centre. Handovers from the studio to OB locations and back again are similarly consistently managed through interactions that explicitly pass the floor to the relevant speaker, whether that is a correspondent at a constituency count, an outgoing Member of Parliament or Dimbleby back in the studio.

A brief comparison with earlier election night broadcasts in Britain will make clear the dexterity with which television had learnt, by the time of the 1997 programme, to deal with spatial fragmentation and with the intricate set of relations between remote sites which is entailed. Early election nights had their hands full managing the transition from the studio to OB locations at all; the kind of tight control over the arcs and circuits of communication which reveals itself in the 1997 broadcast would have been beyond their scope. While the 1955 General Election coverage, for example, featured a number of cuts to places other than the studio – Transport House, the then Labour Party headquarters; Conservative headquarters at Abbey House; New College Oxford, where two historians sat

---

[4] *Radio Times*, 26 April–2 May 1997.

in easy chairs in a college room discussing the results; Crosshands, in Wales, for interviews with a miner and with the Liberal candidate – handovers between these sites and Richard Dimbleby in the studio were not interactive in the way in which they would later become. Dimbleby, certainly, signposted each handover with an explanatory preface ('now we're going to pay another visit out'), and individuals at OB locations would return the favour ('and now back once again to Richard Dimbleby'); but the possibility of an interaction between the anchor and a remote correspondent would appear to be ruled out by the chanciness of the connection. On some occasions, for instance, Dimbleby announced an upcoming cut to elsewhere, only for the screen to turn black; on others, the return to the studio ('and back to Richard Dimbleby in the studio') was accompanied by a temporary loss of both image and sound before television found its feet again. The tight control over the vector of communication between the television event and the audience at home was similarly absent. In 1997, only David Dimbleby, ostensibly, is permitted a direct address to the viewer; other presenters, such as Paxman, must route their remarks via the anchor. In 1955, seemingly, the institutional voice of the BBC could deliver itself via a number of different speakers. Both interviewers at OB locations and analysts in the studio would appear to be licensed to direct their gaze to camera and their remarks directly to the viewer, with no apparent requirement that they address their remarks through the mediation of the anchor.

Flash forward to 1992, and many of the mechanisms for the management of spatial fragmentation are in place; but even here, a mere five years before the 1997 election night, the BBC's mastery of space looks erratic in places. Whilst the 1992 programme contains some of the same tightly controlled elements as 1997 – a sequence of down-the-line interviews with reporters at party headquarters, for example, which displays the same use of framing and the same shifts from mediated to 'unmediated' footage as I described earlier – there are also a number of moments, particularly later on in the evening, where the 1992 broadcast seems overwhelmed by the chaos of the spatial fragmentation it is attempting to synthesize. An interview between the reporter Michael Buerk and leader of the Liberal Democrats Paddy Ashdown in Yeovil, for example, is interrupted in mid-sentence by a voiceover from David Dimbleby announcing a cut to Glasgow Govan, where a result is imminently expected in the constituency of Jim Sillars, deputy leader of the Scottish National Party; at the end of the Sillars declaration, the programme cuts directly back to Yeovil, to the accompaniment of a further studio voiceover ('All right, well we leave Glasgow Govan and with apologies to Paddy Ashdown we go back to him and Michael Buerk with the news that Jim Sillars has lost that seat'), and subsequently, again with a Dimbleby voiceover, back to Govan ('We go back to Govan where Jim Sillars is speaking'). Whilst the voiceovers here impart a measure of coherence to the spatial transitions, there are no intervening establishing shots from the studio in the manner of the 1997 broadcast; and there are other moments where competing news values conspire to overwhelm the BBC's ability to manage the flood of information from simultaneous elsewheres. Thus the 1992 broadcast cuts directly from Conservative MP Norman Lamont's acceptance speech at Kingston to Chris

Patten at Bath, with a Dimbleby voiceover contextualizing the cut only after
it has happened ('Norman Lamont at his count in Kingston and we're going
we're keeping an eye on Bath'); and a few minutes later the broadcast cuts
to an outside location which Dimbleby initially identifies as Monklands East,
Labour MP John Smith's seat, only to correct himself subsequently ('This is
Monklands West, I'm sorry'). Chris Lowe's face-to-face with Kenneth Baker is
unceremoniously cut short in mid-sentence for a return to Peter Sissons in the
studio ('Now with me is another party chairman, Cecil Parkinson'); and shortly
thereafter Dimbleby interrupts the Conservative MP Kenneth Clarke, during their
down-the-line interview, to go to Wallasey ('Mr Clarke, thank you very much,
we go to Wallasey where we think Lynda Chalker is in trouble'). The programme
then cuts almost immediately to Bath, for footage of Chris Patten in mid-interview
surrounded by a crowd, and as Patten turns away from the cameras, cuts back to
Wallasey where the declaration has taken place in the interim, to be missed by
the BBC. Only at this latter point does a Dimbleby voiceover attempt to bring
events back under control ('Well we interrupted the Wallasey result to hear Chris
Patten there, Lynda Chalker has lost this seat in Wallasey ...').

In a piece in which he discusses the coverage of elections in America, Hallin
argues for a shift over the last several decades to a 'much more mediated' style
of news presentation, involving such phenomena as the treatment of candidates'
speeches as 'raw material to be taken apart, combined with other sounds and
images, and reintegrated into a new narrative' (1993: 137). One of the reasons
for this transformation, he suggests, is technological development in the sense of
the 'evolution of technical culture more broadly, of television "know-how", and
a television aesthetic' (1993: 139). Television journalists are, in other words,
'better at using the medium today' (1993: 140). The tightly controlled and
mediated presentation of live material in *Election 97*, slick and seamless even by
comparison with its immediate predecessor, is similarly suggestive of the rapid
development of highly sophisticated strategies for managing space.

6.3   Mediated Encounters

As the discussion in the previous section has demonstrated, election night
coverage in the UK involves a wide range of remote locations, which the
programme must integrate into the live flow of the broadcast if it is to deliver
a coherent account of what is going on. In this, the televising of British
General Elections differs from the way in which American Presidential Elections
are covered. While the latter, both on American and on British television,
certainly feature a number of remote places – Democratic and Republican party
headquarters, for example, and party rallies – the scope for encompassing large
numbers of remote sites within the broadcast is limited by the different nature
of the event. In Britain, the significant moments of election nights occur at each
constituency when the candidates are lined up and a returning officer formally
declares who has won the constituency. All polls close nationwide at the same
time, and the timing of the results is dictated simply by the speed at which

votes are counted in different places. In America, by contrast, with its several time zones, polls close over several hours; and as the polls close, the American networks 'call' the results for those states based on exit poll predictions and early raw vote tabulations. The significant moments, in other words, which serve as the points of departure for the elaborative scenarios of pundits and prognosticators, are not moments that are actually occurring in some simultaneous elsewhere, but are rather, as one journalist put it some days after the 2000 Presidential Election, 'phantasmagoria … media predictions based on scanty "exit polls"'.[5] American election night broadcasts, as a consequence, have nowhere to go, so to speak: there are no definitive moments on the night in remote locations to which television can 'take' its audience. Such moments as the television event produces it must construct from its own calls and from the excitement which these generate (Marriott, 2007).

In Britain, as we have seen, the case is otherwise. The key moments of the night, which television must capture if it is to deliver the event, will be transpiring at some determinate instant in some simultaneous elsewhere; it is up to the broadcaster to ensure that cameras are there at the right time so that the appropriate feed is available for the control gallery to select. There is, however, more of a similarity between the two events than this account might suggest. *Election 97* did not simply relay the diverse remote locations in which the events of the night were unfolding; it also sought to bring them, at key moments, into a dialectical relationship with each other. Seen from this perspective, election night in Britain, too, involves a construction of moments which would not exist were television not present to synthesize them.

Election 97 made much of its capacity to bring disparate elements of the absent world to the viewer in the moment in which they were unfolding. As David Dimbleby made clear at the top of the *Election 97* broadcast, the programme would seek to be 'in' or 'at' as many of these locations as possible:

> It is at any rate going to be a very very exciting political night. We are already at all the places that matter, the count at Sedgefield for Tony Blair, his Labour club, with the Tories in Huntingdon, with the Liberal Democrats in Yeovil. We'll be following the party leaders, we'll be at the party headquarters, we'll be at the key marginal seats where the battles are being fought and people are discovering whether they've lost or won.

> And we're going to be in hundreds and hundreds of places, well perhaps that's a slight exaggeration but at least over a hundred places throughout the United Kingdom. There they all are waiting for us now, and we'll be going to them through the night with reporters going to the counts and hearing the story uh when when it as it as it comes through.

These opening remarks establish the taken-for-granted electronic conjuring trick which the BBC was attempting to pull off in the live space of the broadcast. Dimbleby and other presenters would be in the studio, but the broadcast – 'we' – would also be in or at 'hundreds and hundreds' of other places. To think about the way in which television constructs this kind of event, then, is to think about

---

[5] Ed Vulliamy (2000), 'Rollercoaster Ride to the White House', *The Observer*. Available at http:// talk.workunlimited.co.uk/print/0,,4089984-103632,00.html (accessed 8 June 2007).

the way in which the event is assembled by means of a synthesis between what is going on in these diverse OB locations and what is going on in the studio.

It is when we come to consider the ways in which participants are brought into a mediated encounter with each other that we begin to see the complexity and intricacy of the programme's management of space. As an initial example we can consider the following: Barbara Follett, a Labour Party modernizer, has just won a seat, and she and her husband, along with a number of supporters, are attempting to open a large bottle of champagne. The studio screen shows a number of unsuccessful attempts to remove the cork, to the accompaniment of increasing hilarity from Dimbleby and others in the studio. The programme cuts to a BBC reporter, who is about to interview the Labour politician Robin Cook at the Royal Festival Hall. 'Nobody's gonna call Ken and Barbara champagne socialists ever again after that performance,' says Cook. The inference is clear. Cook is able to comment on the unfolding television event because he was watching it on a screen at the Festival Hall shortly before he, in turn, comes to feature as a participant within that same event. Material from one live segment of the programme has here become instantly available to be talked through in the next.

As a further and more structured set of examples, we can take the following series of interviews with Conservative politicians from the early part of the evening. Michael Heseltine, the Deputy Prime Minister, was interviewed on BBC Radio 4 and, in the absence of any results as yet, had provided a preliminary formulation of what was to become a central topic for both interviewers and interviewees over the night: why the Conservatives were going to lose the election.

> It doesn't look good. But then it did not look good at the last election at this stage … if the polls are right and we have actually lost then there have to be a lot of questions asked and a lot of answers produced.
>
> (Michael Heseltine, Radio 4; quoted in Cathcart, 1997: 12)

This initial formulation was transmuted into a question posed in the studio by the presenter Jeremy Paxman, at this stage of the evening face-to-face with the Conservative MP and Defence Secretary Michael Portillo:

JP   Michael Portillo, are you ready to drink hemlock yet?

MP   Certainly not. Er one result doesn't make the General Election result. In any case, uh I will just comment on each result as they come in. It's not for me to make uh any statement about the overall position.

JP   Michael Heseltine says you need to uh analyse where you went wrong.

MP   Well of course uh if it doesn't work out well for us tonight we would have to do that, er what I hope we would do is do it in a considered, measured way over a period of time, emphasizing the need for unity within the party and not jumping to conclusions.

The BBC cut shortly thereafter to Derbyshire South, where the Europhile MP Edwina Currie was interviewed on-site by a reporter. In a discussion in which she was remarkably frank about the defects and problems of her own party, she commented that 'the electorate has never voted for a party that is antagonistic to Europe'. This face-to-face interaction was followed in quick succession by a number of down-the-line interviews. First, the MP Stephen Dorrell was interviewed in a live two-way with Jeremy Paxman:

JP   Do you agree with Edwina Currie that it was the divisions in your party and particularly the behaviour of the Eurosceptics that did for you?

SD   I don't accept by any means that the result of the election has yet been decided or at least that it's yet known. Uh I do agree with what I heard Michael Portillo saying earlier on in your programme, namely that uh a party that presents a united face to the electorate is a party that strengthens its claim to their support ...

Immediately afterwards came Malcolm Rifkind at his constituency in Edinburgh. Paxman's question:

JP   Just so we're clear that the cabinet is at least united on uh this matter, you do share the view of Stephen Dorrell and Michael Portillo that what damaged you, what did for you, was the fact that you were divided?

Finally David Dimbleby conducted a remote interview with Michael Heseltine, whose original radio comment was used to spark off the sequence:

DD   Michael Portillo says that it's disunity that was the problem for the Tory party. Would you agree with that?

This material – and much else like it, over the course of the evening – provides us with ample evidence of the way in which the broadcast articulates different remote locations and brings them into an interactively-structured relationship with each other. In this way, the television event begins to construct itself self-referentially out of metadiscursive exchanges in and between spatially-dispersed locations as encounters with successive sites impact in turn upon each other.

   This is not simply a matter of the way in which presenters used the material of previous exchanges to cue the next interview. We can note in this respect Stephen Dorrell's evasion of the question about Edwina Currie, in which he himself turned instead to what he had 'heard Michael Portillo saying earlier on in your programme'. This is a phenomenon that occurred over and over as the television event unfolded. When Conservative MP Gillian Shepherd was asked by Dimbleby why the Conservatives were suffering 'this devastating defeat', she began her reply by commenting on the 'various theories' which had been 'put forward on your programmes during the course of the evening'. The next two examples again show MPs picking up on earlier elements of the television event in which they themselves were now participating. Here is Labour MP Jack Straw in a live two-way with Jeremy Paxman, making reference to an earlier down-the-line interview between Gordon Brown at his own count in Scotland and David Dimbleby in the studio:

JP   Jack Straw, are you expecting to be Home Secretary?

JS   Well my uh answer to that is the same as the one you received from Gordon Brown about half an hour ago is that uh we'll wait and see ...

Similarly, Gillian Shepherd's allusions to Michael Portillo in the next example are references to his speech and demeanour when he lost his seat at Enfield Southgate some few minutes earlier:

DD   What do you make of the results so far?

GS   Well clearly as uh Michael Portillo said it's an enormously disappointing night for the government, for the Conservative Party. It's a particular blow that Michael has uh so narrowly lost his seat, he will be enormously missed and I so admired the typically graceful and elegant and indeed generous way uh in which he just spoke ...

Participants even privileged remotely acquired information over material available in their own immediate context of co-presence. The correspondent Lance Price, for example, in a live two-way with David Dimbleby from Michael Portillo's count at Enfield Southgate, referred back not to a discussion he has himself had face-to-face with Portillo but rather to what he had heard Portillo say earlier in the studio 'on this programme' before Portillo left for his constituency. In all of these cases the speakers were talking about events in sites remote from their own, which they had access to via monitors in their own location.

Most revealing of all from this point of view is the footage of Michael Portillo losing his seat at Enfield Southgate, a sequence which brings together in a moment of remarkable timing and editing the self-referential properties of the broadcast. As votes for the Labour candidate, Stephen Twigg, are read out by the returning officer and it becomes clear that Portillo has been defeated, the BBC begins to cut to a number of other remote locations for reaction shots.

Here is what is available to be seen by the viewer, in rapid succession on the screen: the candidates lining up on the stage to hear the declaration; the Conservative MP John Redwood, observing intently at his count in Wokingham; the Conservative MP Gillian Shepherd, watching a television screen at her own count in Norfolk South West; Redwood again; Labour supporters cheering at the Royal Festival Hall; Shepherd again; then back to the declaration at Enfield Southgate. The whole is accompanied by ambient sound from Enfield Southgate and by a Dimbleby voiceover from the studio:

> Well look at the face of Gillian Shepherd listening to these results coming through, watching the screen, and John Redwood in Wokingham. Michael Portillo has lost the seat, Labour celebrates at the Festival Hall as the Thatcher favourite, one of the bastards in the Cabinet as John Major called him, he was accused of plotting last time for the leadership, is defeated by young Stephen Twigg.

This is a remarkable televisual moment, particularly when viewed in terms of the intricate and interconnected transformations of space that are involved in the construction of the sequence. As with the other examples I have been considering here, what is at stake in this instance is the embedding into the event of reactions to the event. This time, however, the phenomenon is manifested on an unparalleled scale, as the live feed from Portillo's declaration is fed back to the BBC, from where it is transmitted to be watched by Redwood, Shepherd and the Labour Party supporters at the Royal Festival Hall. Their multiple and separate acts of watching are fed back to us in turn. Individuals are thus *at one and the same moment* consumers of the television event – watching it from their own particular parts of the country – and participants in it. The circumstances of production and reception collide here in the instantaneous *now* of the live broadcast.

The simultaneity of transmission and reception in this case permits the intersection of action and reaction in the flow of the live broadcast even as it generates the circumstances in which a response to an event can instantaneously occur. Television here constructs the situation even as it produces and transmits it, so that the broadcast does not simply re-present some diegetic event which is occurring independently in the 'real' world; instead, the event which is constitutive of the narrative is unfolding dynamically through the electronic mediation of the live broadcast in the encounters between spatially-simultaneous sites. As participants in turn are confronted both with the event of Portillo's defeat and with the reactions – of others, and of themselves – to that event, so the instantaneity of electronic communication brings spatially-dispersed sites into a dialectical relationship with each other. What an examination of the Portillo declaration reveals, crucially, is the dynamic nature of the process, the way in which information flows not just from the centre to the periphery but rather backwards and forwards in a dialectical interplay, not only impacting upon the periphery but also generating the television event itself.

How did this intricate management of space compare to the 1992 election night programme? Just as the 1997 broadcast features Portillo's defeat as its emblematic moment, so a focal point in 1992 was the defeat of the then-Chairman of the Conservative Party, Chris Patten. Whilst these two episodes stand in a different relationship to the overall narrativization of the evening's events – Patten had a majority of less than 1,500 and represented a relatively rare moment of defeat for the Conservatives in an evening where they otherwise held on to power – the place they occupy in the structure of the broadcast is otherwise alike. The Patten declaration, for example, shared with its successor the insertion of reaction shots into the footage of the event unfolding, although in this case the participants stood in a more contingent relationship to each other. As votes for the Liberal Democrat candidate were announced and the crowd broke into cheers, the broadcast showed, in an overlapping window in the top right hand corner, the Conservative MP Kenneth Clarke at his Rushcliffe constituency listening intently with his hand cupped over his ear and then the Labour MP Jack Cunningham at the back of a crowd at his count in Copeland, accompanied by a voiceover from David Dimbleby:

Chris Patten has lost this seat. Jack Cunningham in Copeland listening.

Like *Election 97*, the 1992 broadcast also featured references by participants to the unfolding event. Such references were, however, uncommon. After Patten's defeat, the reporter Chris Lowe, face-to-face with former Conservative Party Chairman Kenneth Baker, opened the discussion with the following comment:

> Mr Baker, you just watched Chris Patten's defeat. You winced.

This remark aside, there were only occasional metadiscursive references in the 1992 broadcast. The following two extracts both involve endorsements from Labour MPs (Brian Gould in the first case and John Prescott in the second) of remarks made by John Cole, one of the BBC's political commentators, in the studio:

> I think we would very much go with the point that John Cole made a moment ago ...
>
> I think there's a lot to be done uh a lot to be said for what uh John Cole has just said there ...

There was also only one additional reaction shot besides the footage of the Patten declaration, when Paddy Ashdown, leader of the Liberal Democrat Party, was seen watching his party's first victory of the night from his constituency in Yeovil. Encounters between the studio and remote individuals in *Election 92* were thus overwhelmingly constituted as one-to-one and relatively isolated interactions.

6.4   Conclusion: Simultaneous Elsewheres

The intercutting of action and reaction, of event and response to event which manifests itself in the Portillo sequence represents not a moment of serendipity for the BBC – a fortuitous bringing-together of the dramatis personae at the critical moment – but rather a felicitous manifestation of the complex procedures for the management of spatial fragmentation which went into the programme. It was this systematic attention to detail, the way in which the broadcast was 'always already ahead of itself' (Scannell, 1996: 152), which delivered, too, the sequence's self-referential structure, with the BBC alerting its OB crews in advance in 1997 to the desirability of 'pairings' ('The idea is that when key events happen, we pair them with shots of people watching'). As the BBC put it: 'One glum face caught unawares can capture a mood better than any interview'.[6]

How did the programme arrange events so that it would have access to such pairings in 1997? The BBC not only was on the look-out for pairings; it had also stressed, in its documentation, that both reporters and interviewees should watch the broadcast and if possible 'pick up' from the minutes preceding their segment.

> Remember guests will be asked to comment on what they have seen and heard ... so it is important that they have the appropriate facilities and atmosphere to listen, watch and respond.

Although the BBC's declared intention in this instance was simply to enhance what it saw as the 'cohesiveness' of the programme, the outcome was something

---

[6]Information on production strategies is taken from the BBC's Outside Broadcast guide for *Election 97*, and from discussions with the programme editor.

more: the phenomenal complexity of the spatio-temporal dynamics of the event as it has revealed itself here.

Critical to any hermeneutic account of the phenomenology of this kind of event is the dialectical interplay between simultaneous elsewheres. In such instances, the event cannot be viewed, experientially, as simply a re-construction by television of an occurrence or series of occurrences in the real world. Rather, it is constructed in a dynamic relationship between centre and periphery by and through remote encounters between participants and places. Seen from this perspective, the phenomenology of the event is quite extraordinarily intricate: not just engendered by some series of activities at some remote locale or locales which television then re-fashions spatially and temporally into the stuff of the live television event, but generated rather via the penetration of locales into other locales, and of events in one locale into other locales, through the electronic mediation of the live broadcast.

7

Time, Space and Catastrophe

7.1 The Live Coverage of Catastrophes

I suggested in Chapter 5 that there are two key characteristics of live television which impact upon the way in which the event is realized: its delivery of a range of different locales and moments, and its real-time multiple mediations of the world in which stuff is happening.

In Chapter 6 we examined some of the consequences of these characteristics for one particular kind of live occasion, election night, where a complex set of dialectical relationships was established between the centre of the event (the studio from which the live event was spoken) and its peripheries (the constituency counts and other locales).

One significant element in television's live performance of *Election 97* was the availability and distribution of personal media such as pagers and mobile phones. There were several references in the broadcast to the use of such media, as the following anecdote will demonstrate:

> Next came Hartlepool, and another juicy moment in the interplay of screen with life. Here we watched Labour's campaign director joking with onlookers at his own count. Dimbleby observed: 'Peter Mandelson who apparently escaped a terrible car accident yesterday. He's the man who really constructed the whole of this campaign. He was responsible for every twist and turn of manipulation. He's known as the Prince of Darkness.' As we heard these words, we saw Mandelson reach into a pocket, pull out a pager and look down to read from the little screen. Dimbleby was watching. 'And there he is, looking at the pager with messages coming through – probably saying, "You're on BBC1. Smile." They control things so closely.' Mandelson did not smile.

> (Cathcart, 1997: 15)

In such situations, local contexts of co-presence may be deluged with information from electronically mediated sources. Individuals in remote locations may be accessing other sites via fax or telephone, receiving pager messages sent by other spatially-dispersed individuals or watching the unfolding of remote events on a screen or a monitor; and they may, furthermore, be communicating at a distance with the studio for the further perusal of both present and non-present others who may, like themselves, be watching television, receiving messages and conferring in turn, all the while drawing this flood of information from disparate simultaneous sources into their understanding of the current state of play. It is this extensive availability of remote encounters with absent others which draws participants into the complex and dialectical communicative framework which I outlined in the previous chapter.

In this final chapter I will continue to explore the interactional possibilities which are opened up by the development and spatial distribution of electronic forms of communication. My focus here, as in other chapters, will be on the phenomenology of the live television event; and I will be arguing here for a distinct phenomenological shift in the nature of the event.

My concern in this chapter will be those live events which have been referred to elsewhere as 'news events' (Dayan and Katz, 2003), 'happenings' (Scannell, 1999), 'crises' (Doane, 1990; Nimmo and Combs, 1985) or 'catastrophes' (Doane, 1990). Such events are of particular interest for a consideration of live television because of the way in which they erupt spontaneously, taking over the schedules. All live television events, as I argued in Chapter 4, are *atelic*, inasmuch as they come into being in the moment of transmission and reception. Classic media events, however, generally afford television a considerable period of time in which to 'forestructure' the occasion (Scannell, 1999: 29), and as a consequence broadcasters are able to demonstrate, at their best, a fairly flawless mastery of the occasion, with smooth transitions from one shot to the next and an integral and unobtrusive voiceover commentary which serves both to contextualize the image and to anticipate what will come next. The case is otherwise with the breaking news story or catastrophe. Flung into the middle of a situation which may or may not be ongoing, may or may not be about to develop in unanticipated directions, the broadcaster must scramble to provide coverage of the situation and to construct a narrative whose substance must be shaped in the real time of transmission and reception. In such a situation, the ability to communicate rapidly and in real time with the peripheries of the event is crucial if the broadcaster is to establish and frame what is going on.

I will argue in this chapter that the increasingly complex connectivity of the world has had an extraordinarily far-reaching impact upon the phenomenology of live disaster coverage. I will suggest, furthermore, that we can trace this impact, in part at least, to the growing mobility of electronic forms of communication. In what follows, I will examine this question via a consideration of the communicative circuits which arise at the moment of breaking news.

7.2 The Catastrophic Event: JFK and 9/11

In the aftermath of the attack on the World Trade Center in 2001, the event was compared – in the suddenness with which it burst upon the world, in its capacity to hold huge television audiences enthralled for hours or days at a time, in the demands which it made upon broadcasters – to another, earlier event. As the NBC anchor Tom Brokaw put it: 'It was very much like the Kennedy assassination' (Gilbert et al., 2002: 171). A close inspection of the live television coverage in 2001 and 1963, however, reveals significant differences between these two events.

We can start to consider these differences via an examination of the live talk produced by the anchors on each occasion, with particular reference to the question of *evidentiality* (Anderson, 1986; Bybee, 1985; Chafe, 1986; Chung and

Timberlake, 1985; Willett, 1988), the way in which speakers indicate the source for their statements. Willett (1988: 57) distinguishes *direct evidence* (garnered from an individual's own perceptual access to an event) from *indirect evidence* (which must be either inferred from a situation or gleaned second- or third-hand from the reports of others). This will prove to be a useful distinction in examining these two events. A brief consideration, for example, of the live US coverage on NBC in the early hours after Kennedy's assassination makes it clear that the anchors' source for the information which they are relaying to the audience is entirely *indirect*, inasmuch as it is based on the reports of others:

> **The report is** that the President is in very critical condition.

> The President is seriously wounded. **This information comes from** Senator Ralph Yarborough.

> A policeman **has told** Bob that he heard, the policeman heard that it was a high-powered rifle.

> **There is this** from Dallas … President Kennedy has been given blood transfusions.

> **The word** still is that the President is in very serious condition, **the reports say** he is in critical condition.

> Just a moment Bob I'm going to interrupt for a **bulletin that the Associated Press has moved** from Dallas.

> So that is the story. The President of the United States is dead. The new President of the United States is Lyndon Johnson … President Kennedy, **we are now informed**, was shot in the right temple. It was a simple matter of a bullet right through the head, **said** Doctor George Berkeley, the White House medical officer.

The following two utterances provide more detailed examples. The first disclosure of Kennedy's death is couched in terms which repeatedly remind the audience of the sources of the anchors' second- and third-hand knowledge (the Associated Press; two priests at the Dallas Memorial Hospital), and reiterate the epistemological status of the information (unconfirmed, partial) and its status as hearsay. The second statement, from a Dallas-based NBC affiliate some minutes later, operates in a similar vein.

> **Here is a flash from the Associated Press** dateline Dallas. Two priests who were with President Kennedy **say** he is dead of bullet wounds. There is no further confirmation but **this is what we have on a flash basis from the Associated Press**. Two priests in Dallas who were with President Kennedy **say** he is dead of bullet wounds. There is no further confirmation. **This is the only word we have** indicating that the President may in fact have lost his life. **It is just moved on the Associated Press wires** from Dallas. The two priests were called to the hospital to administer the last rites of the Roman Catholic church and **it is from them we get the word** that the President has died, that the bullet wound inflicted on him as he rode in the motorcade through downtown Dallas have been fatal. We would remind you **there is no official confirmation of this from any source as yet**.

> Substantiating this but not confirming it is **a report** about five minutes ago by the Dallas police department to all of its officers that the President had died. Some three five minutes later **the Associated Press flashed** that two priests at the hospital **say** the President is dead.

The same kinds of 'quotative' (Chung and Timberlake, 1985) or 'hearsay' (Chafe, 1986: 268) evidentials turn up in the live 9/11 coverage, as these extracts from NBC in 2001 will demonstrate:

> Just to recap if you're just joining us you're looking at dramatic pictures of New York's World Trade Center in Lower Manhattan, where a short time ago **we are told** that a plane crashed into the upper floors of the westernmost tower.

> Right now **we're getting information**, Al, that it was a small commuter plane.

> Just a few minutes ago **we're told** that a plane, **some reports** are that it was a small commuter plane …

> It's a 737, **we're now being told**.

Such utterances are in the minority in 2001, however, particularly in the early stages of the event when authoritative comments from external sources were thin on the ground. What we find instead is comment after comment where the warranty for the speakers' assertions is provided not on the basis of reports from others but rather via their own (mediated) view of what is transpiring:

> There was another one **we just saw we just saw** another one **we just saw** another one apparently go another plane just flew into the second tower … **we just saw** on live television as a second plane flew into the second tower of the World Trade Center.

> (Fox News)

> We just **saw** a plane circling the building a second ago on the shot right before that.

> (NBC)

> We **have another view** now of that plane slamming into the second building, **look** at it, it's coming in from the side, coming low, hitting the building about in the middle. Folks, you **see** the pictures, it **looks** like Hollywood but this is real.

> (CNN)

> We're gonna look for that tape one more time, we're gonna re-rack the tape here and see if we can't **see** um a plane, yeah, we **see** it right now, we **see** a plane right now coming in and impacting on what **would appear** to be the north side of that tower.

> (CBS)

> What I wanna do is **take a look** at that airplane in slow motion, it **looks** like a jet aircraft.

> (MSNBC)

> There's there is a further there is a further dramatic explosion **we're just witnessing** there we **saw** a plane a a small plane passing by and there **seems** to be a further explosion.

> (BBC News 24)

How might we account for this difference between the two events, which we might characterize as an overall shift from indirect to direct sources of evidence? We might, first of all, attribute it to the different moments at which television began its coverage. In the case of 9/11, the live transmissions had already commenced by the time the second tower was attacked, and the anchors were therefore in a position to comment on what they could see transpiring in real time on the studio monitors. The shooting of Kennedy, by contrast, was a telic event which had already concluded by the time the live breaking news broadcasts went on air, and there was therefore no possibility of viewing or commenting on it live.

This explanation, however, will not take us very far. Although the shooting itself had already happened in 1963 by the time NBC and the other broadcasters went on air, it is clear from the extracts above that the ramifications of the event – was Kennedy alive or dead? Who had shot him? – were still in the process of making themselves known. Were such an incident to occur now, live footage from the scene – the hospital, Dealey Plaza, the relevant police precincts – would clearly be on the screen, even if this could only serve as a strictly uninformative backdrop to the anchor's voiceover, as in this extract from the BBC's live coverage of the (similarly telic) de Menezes shooting in 2005:

> So what is happening now? **We we can see** this this street in front of the station, I presume it's in front of the station, **we can see** a bus that's parked there, no traffic but people, some people on the pavement.

(BBC News 24)

A more useful explanation can be offered by considering the technology which television had at its disposal in 1963. We can note, first of all, that there were no live cameras in Dealey Plaza when the President was shot; and in the absence of live cameras, there would be an inevitable and lengthy delay before shooting could commence. Live television broadcasting, in 1963, required considerable planning. Coaxial cable had to be laid in advance, or microwave relays set up; television cameras, furthermore, required a couple of hours to warm up sufficiently to operate.[1] Affiliates of two of the networks – ABC and CBS – had set up live shots at the Dallas Trade Mart, where the President had been due to have lunch, and so those networks were able to deliver live coverage from there; but there could be no live transmission either from Dealey Plaza or from the Dallas Memorial Hospital where he was taken. There were no live radio commentators in Dealey Plaza either, although an ostensibly live broadcast ('We can't see who has been hit if anybody's been hit, but apparently something is wrong here, something is terribly wrong') was in circulation for many years afterwards, produced by a Dallas KBOX commentator after the event as a re-creation of the event, complete with the sounds of sirens and gunfire. It would be several hours before film, still wet from developing, began to appear on television screens, a somewhat macabre combination of material shot earlier in the day of an apparently relaxed and smiling Kennedy in Fort Worth joking to the cameras about the popularity of his wife, and raw footage of members of the public milling around Dealey Plaza or keeping vigil outside the hospital.

---

[1] http://www.museum.tv/archives/etv/K/htmlK/kennedyjf/kennedyjf.htm (accessed 10 July 2005).

Only one film of the assassination was to come the networks' way, and they declined to purchase it. A Dallas clothing manufacturer called Abraham Zapruder had captured the assassination of the President on his super 8 camera and sold the footage to *Life Magazine*. NBC and ABC, offered the film some days after the event, viewed it and decided not to use it, on the grounds that it was 'too dramatic' and not 'the thing for home television'. 'The inside of a man's brain being outside', as one NBC producer put it, was too awful to broadcast (Love, 1965: 83–84). The film would not appear on American television until 1975.

This absence of live footage led to a radically different form of coverage when compared to more recent live breaking news broadcasts. Once again we can consider the NBC broadcast here. To examine the broadcast now is to watch the three anchors – Frank McGee, Chet Huntley and Bill Ryan – sitting behind a desk facing the camera with a blank wall behind them, addressing the audience at home, turning to talk with one another, speaking into a telephone, listening to messages on earpieces or picking up pieces of paper which are placed on the desk in front of them by individuals off-screen. Occasionally one of them will prop up on the desk a hastily developed photograph of a hale and hearty Kennedy snapped earlier in the day, and attempt to orient it so that the image can be picked up by the camera. Throughout these activities, these anchors are relaying information as it comes in: from the wire services, whose periodic updates are read out on air as soon as they are placed in front of them or received via their earpieces, and from the NBC correspondent Bob McNeill, who was with the presidential motorcade in Dallas and who has gone on to the Dallas Memorial Hospital. McNeill is phoning in regular reports which cannot be heard on air for most of the early stages of the broadcast and which must therefore be repeated verbatim by Frank McGee, who is talking to him on the telephone. At intervals a hand will enter the frame and attempt to set up a device on the desk which will permit McNeill's voice to be heard live on air. As this device functions only intermittently, McGee must constantly break off either to allow McNeill to be heard or to start repeating his words verbatim when it becomes clear that the device isn't working.

It is hardly surprising, given this set of circumstances, that the discourse produced in the studio in 1963 should be almost entirely metadiscursive: it is talk about talk, as the extracts above have demonstrated, because talk – the words of others – is by and large all that the broadcaster has at its disposal. 9/11 could not be more different in this respect. As we saw in Chapter 3, all of the major American networks and cable news channels were airing live footage from New York within five minutes of the first plane hitting the North Tower of the World Trade Center. By the time this tower collapsed just before 10.30 a.m. Eastern Time, all of the channels had agreed to pool footage (Gilbert et al., 2002: 125), and this footage was also on offer in the form of live feeds to affiliate stations and other broadcasters worldwide. Over the course of several hours, around the globe, live images of the World Trade Center and re-racked footage of key moments of the day's events dominated television screens.

To watch the early stages of the live coverage of 9/11 is to become aware of one important consequence of this superabundance of raw footage: a preoccupation with the moment of witnessing. Several of the broadcasters – NBC, for instance, and CNN – positioned key personnel on rooftops, where they could serve simultaneously as anchors and eyewitnesses. This sense of direct witness emerges as a powerful element in their commentary. Here, for example, is Aaron Brown from CNN, live on a rooftop as the North Tower collapses:

> There has just been a huge explosion **we can see** uh a billowing smoke rising and I can't I'll tell you that **I can't see** that second tower but y there was a cascade of sparks and fire and now there's **it looks** almost like a mushroom cloud explosion this huge billowing smoke in the second tower this was the second of the two towers hit and I you **know I cannot see** behind that smoke obviously...

In this extract the quotative forms which occurred so regularly in the live 1963 coverage ('the reports say ...'; 'we are informed ...') have given way entirely to 'experiential' (Chung and Timberlake, 1985) or 'attested' (Willett, 1988) evidentials ('we can see'; 'it looks'), which make it clear that the speaker's comments are warranted by his own direct experience of the world. Nor are the anchors – whether they are in the studio watching what is happening on their monitors, or out on the rooftop seeing for themselves – the only individuals who are implicated in this moment of witnessing. The experience – in a mediated form – is also repeatedly offered to the remote audience, who are exhorted again and again to look and see for themselves:

> We have some remarkable pictures coming in from New York which we can go to now and they show us that one of the world's tallest buildings right in the heart of the business district of Manhattan, the World Trade Center, appears to be on fire. **As you can see**, something has clearly happened towards the top of the building and these are very dramatic live pictures coming into the BBC right now.

> (BBC News 24)

> This just in **you are looking at** obviously a very disturbing live shot there that is the World Trade Center and we have unconfirmed reports this morning that a plane has crashed into one of the towers of the World Trade Center.

> (CNN)

> Just to recap if you're just joining us **you're looking at** dramatic pictures of New York's World Trade Center in Lower Manhattan, where a short time ago we are told that a plane crashed into the upper floors of the westernmost tower. **You can see** a gaping hole, that is on the north side of the building, and **you can see** residual damage on the west side of the building, and **obviously** fires are burning right right now in the World Trade Center.

> (NBC)

How might we think about the phenomenology of these events, about the way in which they are mediated and structured by television so as to offer a particular kind of experience to the audience? The live broadcasts in 2001 offer a number of positions from which the event can be encountered: the direct access to the event which is the domain of broadcast personnel on rooftops overlooking Lower Manhattan; the mediated encounter which is on offer not only to the anchors in the studios but also to the audience at home, who are offered the image as a token of veridicality and invited to position themselves as witnesses to the event in the moment of its unfolding. None of these positions were available in 1963. As we have seen, certain essential elements of the event – the shooting itself, the rapid drive to the hospital – had already transpired by the time television arrived to make sense of them, whilst footage of the others – what was happening at the hospital, in Washington, elsewhere in Dallas – was not accessible live on the air. As a result, the broadcast was unable to offer the audience an encounter with the 'real' of the event; it could not provide the opportunity to witness. What it could do, certainly, was to permit the audience to 'be there' at the moment when the news got out, to witness the moment when the death of the President was announced; but this was the moment when the town crier first reveals the catastrophic, and not the moment of the catastrophe itself as one would encounter it if one were *there*.

This view of the difference between these events opens up an important question, which has to do with the relationship between witnessing and mediation. To watch an event on television is, as I said in Chapter 1, to engage with a representation, inasmuch as we cannot remotely encounter the real. How, then, can this kind of experience be described as a moment of witnessing? For some writers this appears relatively unproblematic. Ellis's view, for instance, that the twentieth century was the 'century of witness' (2000: 9) makes it clear that he regards mediated encounters with events-at-a-distance as sufficient. As he puts it,

> a profound shift has taken place in the way we perceive the world that exists beyond our immediate experience … The acceleration of communications has brought us word of so many events, so many peoples, so many places. We live in an era of information, and photography, film and television have brought us visual evidence. Their quasi-physical documentation of specific moments in specific places has brought us face to face with the great events, the banal happenings, the horrors and the incidental cruelties of our time.

(Ellis, 2000: 9)

Not all writers, however, are prepared to grant remote observers the full set of rights and privileges associated with an immediate encounter with the event. Peters, for example, draws a distinction between the licence to attest to the authenticity of the event which is bestowed upon an individual who was *there*, and what he regards as the second-hand relation to the situation which is held by those who are present at a distance (Peters, 2001: 717). While the latter can claim the status of witnesses who at least are present in time if not in space, they cannot, according to Peters, stand as witnesses to history, precisely because they lack 'privileged (raw, authentic) proximity to facts' (2001: 709). To view an event live, nevertheless, confers upon the individual some kind of a warranty which is altogether denied to those who encounter the event at a later date. Recording, for Peters, is 'the profane zone in which the attitude of witnessing is hardest to sustain' (2001: 720).

As our interest here lies with the phenomenology of the event, however, we should not allow ourselves to be overly concerned with this question. As Peters puts it, during media events 'the borrowed eyes and ears of the media become, however tentatively or dangerously, one's own' (2001: 717). The crucial distinction between the Kennedy coverage and that of 9/11 is that the latter is able to *position* the audience as witnesses to the catastrophic, whether or not this is a status that can be fully warranted by the spatio-temporal characteristics of the situation. Live television, in 2001, operates as an interface, explicitly offering the audience a mediated encounter with the place of the event. In 1963, by contrast, television is essentially a conduit for reports which are being garnered elsewhere and which are then communicated verbally – via the phone, via the wires – to the studio for instantaneous relay to the remote audience. Its mode of dealing with the unexpected is a species of semaphore, receiving and transmitting information as part of a chain of messages whose end point is the viewer at home, with a minimum of interpretative activity along the way.

7.3   Witnessing the Event

In the previous chapter I discussed the spatial intricacy of the live event, the innumerable elsewheres which can be drawn into a dynamic and dialectical relationship with each other in the real time of transmission and reception. Election night serves as an excellent example of the way in which the classic media event, with its long forestructuring period in which to rehearse and refine the substance of the programme, is able to anticipate and engineer felicitous patterns of connectivity between one place and another through the mediation of the studio. We can now continue this investigation of space, place and the live event by considering the manner in which live breaking news works to recruit and integrate the multiplicity of locales which are deemed to be of relevance to the event. As before, we shall see a distinct difference in the management of space and place as we consider more recent events against the backdrop of the 1963 broadcasts. Two related factors will be of particular interest to this discussion: the rise of the 'citizen reporter', and the proliferation of eyewitness accounts in live breaking news.

We can note first of all, with reference to more recent live news stories, both the speed at which details of the event now become known and the transformation in the nature of the sources for the story. In the immediate aftermath of the attack on the London transport system on 7 July 2005, for example, the news broke very fast. Within nine minutes of the first three bombs exploding an image had appeared on a mobile blogger site on the internet (Reeves, 2005: 17). Reuters was able to put out its first report at 9.11 a.m., some 20 minutes after the attacks, a 50-word piece simply noting that there had been a '"bang", possibly power related' and that Liverpool Street station had been closed. Eighteen minutes later they put out a second piece stating that a number of stations had been closed. By this point the Press Association had also put out its first story, and the news had begun to air on the rolling news channels in the UK (Fixter, 2005: 18).

Much of the information acquired and used by the media in the early hours came from people who had been on the scene. Some of these individuals worked for the media or for the press agencies. One Sky News producer, for instance, had been evacuated from Kings Cross and as a result saw the bus explosion in Tavistock Square at 9.47; his report went out live on Sky News three minutes later, swiftly moving the focus of the breaking news story from power surge to deliberate attack (Pike, 2005: 18). Other stories came about as a consequence of media personnel hearing the news on the radio on their way to work. A BBC editor heard on his car radio less than ten minutes after the first explosions that there were disruptions on London Underground; he began reporting to Radio Five Live and BBC News 24 on his mobile phone within minutes, and was speaking live on air as he heard the 'thunderous boom' of the bus explosion at Tavistock Square from a street a few hundred yards away (Pike, 2005: 18).

Many of the early sources, however, were members of the public who had been caught up in the explosions. Again and again it was individuals involved in the morning's events who alerted the media and supplied information and images of the attacks. The London *Evening Standard*, whose first edition of the day at 9.45 a.m. carried the headline 'Bombs on tubes kill commuters', had been alerted to the story in the first instance by a phone call from a contact who was being evacuated from Liverpool Street, and who was running away from the scene of the explosion as he spoke on the phone (Lagan, 2005: 17). The image on the moblogger site, a photo of 'people milling about in front of a train station, with a police car and ambulance in the background', came directly from the mobile phone of a site user and was accompanied by a text message alerting other users to a 'big bang at Liverpool Street' (Reeves, 2005: 17). Another mobile phone image, showing the inside of a tube carriage after one of the explosions, was picked up and prominently displayed by the *Daily Mail* and other newspapers (Reeves, 2005: 17).

Television newsrooms began to receive such pictures and video clips within minutes of the explosions. ITN received over a dozen mobile phone video clips on the first day (Day, 2005: 2). The BBC received 50 images from members of the public by the end of the first hour, and was able to air its first mobile phone sequence of the attacks within 20 minutes of receiving it; its main evening news at 10.00 p.m. featured two mobile phone video clips sent in by members of the public (Day, 2005: 2). Sky News, similarly, aired a mobile phone sequence of one of the bombed tube sites at 1.00 p.m., some 20 minutes after receiving it (Day, 2005: 2).

This flood of eyewitness material was hailed after the event as ushering in a new age of news coverage, marked by the arrival of the 'citizen reporter' (Day, 2005: 2). But the attacks of 7 July were by no means the first occasion on which such 'user-generated material'[2] had had a substantial impact on the reporting of a disaster. In 2004, both the floods in Boscastle in Cornwall and the Asian Tsunami had given rise to a mass of material sent in by members of the public.[3] The live coverage of the attacks on New York in September 2001 was similarly attended by a rapid proliferation of images and information generated by individuals on the ground.

---

[2] Helen Boaden, Director of News, BBC, interviewed in Day (2005).
[3] See note 2.

Gilbert et al.'s (2002) account of the events of 9/11 from the perspective of broadcast journalists provides an extraordinary picture of the way in which the news was gathered in the first hours after it began to break. As with 7/7, much of the information in the early part of the day came from people who were on the scene. Some of these, again, were individuals who worked in television news, who witnessed one or the other of the impacts from the windows of an apartment or an office, or on the ground nearby, or from a news helicopter already in the skies over New York. Others were members of the public who were caught up in the event. One news correspondent mentions seeing 'throngs of people' on the sidewalks talking on their mobile phones, snapping pictures, listening to radios or simply staring at the catastrophe unfolding in front of them (Gilbert et al., 2002: 56).

As with 7/7, many of the images which were broadcast in the early stages of the disaster came directly or indirectly from members of the public (Carey, 2002: 73). Some were out on the streets with video cameras, and either were hired on the spot to film for the day (Gilbert et al., 2002: 26, 37), were paid hard cash to sell their equipment to the professionals who encountered them (2002: 46) or simply handed them over gratis (2002: 157). Others gave or sold footage to the broadcasters. One tape in particular was hawked around the broadcasters by a photo agency and finally sold to the highest bidder, CNN, after the agency claimed that another network was willing to pay $10,000 for it (Gilbert et al., 2002: 215). The tape, shot by two French documentary makers who were on the streets of New York that morning, had captured the moment when the first plane hit the North Tower of the World Trade Center, before the live television coverage began. Further images and video clips appeared on the internet on community-news sites or peer-to-peer networks such as Morpheus, the latter exhorting its users to 'be the media' by helping to ensure that the news would be available to its users (Hu, 2001, cited in Allan, 2002: 127).

The high visibility of events at the World Trade Center also ensured that there was no shortage of eyewitnesses. The first eyewitness accounts aired extraordinarily quickly. On NBC, the first telephone interview with an eyewitness downtown, conducted in voiceover between the witness and an anchor, aired only 15 seconds into the breaking news coverage; a further five eyewitness accounts went out live over the next 15 minutes. A similar picture emerges on most of the other channels. CBS interviewed five eyewitnesses in the first 20 minutes, the first one airing just 30 seconds after coverage commenced; CNN broadcast a string of eyewitness reports in the first 20 minutes, most of them through affiliate stations in New York.

The early minutes of the breaking news coverage of September 11 are full of exhortations to bear witness, as these extracts from NBC will demonstrate:

Can you please tell me what you **saw**?

Can you tell us a little bit more about what you **heard** when you **heard** this explosion, describe it for us.

So Elliot, what can you **see** right now **from your perspective**?

Did you **see**, George, the second plane that just flew into the sec the other trade tower?

Dan, tell me about people on the ground, are you at **a vantage point** where you can **see** what's happening on the ground?

These requests to bear witness are, in turn, readily responded to in the required form by the individuals interviewed:

I just **heard** another very loud bang and a very large plane that might have been a DC9 or a 747 flew past my window and I think it may have hit the Trade Center.

(NBC)

I just **saw** a plane go into the building.

(CBS)

I just **witnessed** a plane that appeared to be cruising in slightly lower than normal altitude and it **appeared** to have crashed into I don't know which tower it is but it hit directly in the middle.

(CNN)

7.4   Covering the World: The de Menezes Story

The live broadcasts on 9/11 are by no means unique in their rapid conjuration of eyewitness accounts. An examination of the live coverage on BBC News 24 in the immediate aftermath of the shooting of Jean Charles de Menezes on 22 July 2005 will make clear the extent to which live breaking news has become dependent, in the early stages of its coverage, on testimony from members of the public concerning what they saw and heard as bystanders to history.

Menezes was shot by police officers on a train standing in Stockwell underground station, having been followed from a building in Tulse Hill, South London, which was under surveillance following a wave of attempted attacks in London the day before. Hard information was in short supply in the immediate aftermath of the shooting: Menezes was shot at around 10 a.m., and it would not be until around 10.45 a.m. that Scotland Yard would issue a bare statement confirming the situation. BBC News 24 filled the intervening time by calling upon witness after witness to provide their version of events. As on 11 September, individuals seem more than happy to comply:

I **saw** I I **saw** an Asian guy he he looked Pakistani ... he he ran onto the train he was hotly pursued by three what I I I just presumed them to be three plain clothes police officers one of them was wielding a black handgun ... I **saw** the gun being fired five times into into the guy.

I was sitting on the uh uh tube train, it hadn't pulled out of the station at this time but the doors were still open. I **heard** um a lot of shouting, get down, get out. I **looked** to my right, I **saw** a chap run onto the onto the train um Asian guy um he ran onto the train sort of [—] he was running so fast he half sort of tripped but he was being pursued by three guys, one had a black handgun in his hand, left hand, uh as he sort of went down two of them sort of dropped onto him to hold him down and the other one fired the gun, I **heard** five shots … I was maybe four or five yards along where this accident happened, I I **watched** it.

It seems clear that eyewitness testimony is central to the BBC's attempts to construct a narrative of the shooting in this case. The anchors, for instance, repeatedly refer to the eyewitness statements in their periodic summation of the breaking news:

> Now let's just remind you of what's been happening at Stockwell underground station over the past now a very dramatic development. **According to eyewitnesses** uh a man leapt the security barriers, ran into the station onto the platform of the Northern Line, jumped onto the train hotly pursued by plain clothes officers who fired five shots into him at close range. Mark Whitby uh **the man who gave us that account** uh was of course on the train five seats away he said from all of this and he described the scene to News 24.

> Now we've got um uh of course **eyewitness accounts** from every single direction this morning from Stockwell, we've had people on the platform we've had people on the train, we've had people outside the station, um let's have a look into what some of those **eyewitnesses** have been seeing and hearing this morning.

> So just to bring you more on that, we've had **a lot of eyewitness accounts** this morning, piecing together what took place after 10 o'clock at uh Stockwell. Um **one eyewitness** Steven Jones was driving past Stockwell tube station when the incident occurred and he joins me now on the line … what did you see?

As this last example demonstrates, the Menezes coverage exhibits precisely the same exhortations to testify as the 9/11 material. Just as the American broadcasters on 9/11 would enquire of their eyewitnesses as to what they had seen and heard, so the BBC anchors in July 2005 called upon their interviewees to deliver an account of their experiences:

> Tell us what you **saw**, Graham.

> Did you **see** the smoking bag, or just the smoking?

> So you **saw** a smoking carriage, other people said they saw the smoke coming from a bag, but you didn't **see** anybody acting suspiciously.

> You talked about a strong smell, **what kind of smell**?

At first glance, this reliance on eyewitness accounts in the early stages of the Menezes story seems hardly surprising. The shooting, as I have said, was a telic event which had already come to pass by the time the rolling news channels commenced their live coverage. It was therefore too late to send cameras to the scene at Stockwell to provide live images of unfolding events other than the routine goings-on outside the underground station. Given these circumstances, the testimony of individuals who were *there* was the closest that television could come to providing its audience with an encounter with the event. As with the 1963 broadcasts, however, the telicity of the event will not entirely suffice as an explanation. The use of multiple eyewitnesses in the early stages of the 9/11 coverage, when the live broadcast was still clearly *in medias res*, would suggest that the phenomenon has not simply to do with the need to find individuals to attest to a situation which television cannot directly deliver. If we examine the

1963 assassination, furthermore, we will find that there is a marked absence of eyewitness testimony in the immediate aftermath of the shooting, despite the telicity of the event.

Given the abundance of direct eyewitnesses to the shooting of the President in 1963, the live broadcasts which followed might seem like exactly the kind of situation in which television might turn to live testimony to furnish an account of what had transpired. The CBS broadcast, however, has no eyewitness statements in the early hours of its live coverage. Over a similar period of time the NBC broadcast has just one, recorded on tape in an interview format by their local affiliate WBAPTV Fort Worth Dallas and played on air during one of their live handovers to the station. This sole interviewee apart, NBC have at their disposal only their own correspondent, Bob McNeill, who was part of the presidential motorcade. McNeill, in other words, stands in the same relation to events as the BBC editor who hears the bus explosion on 7 July 2005, or the various members of the media who are within sight or hearing of the plane impacts on 11 September 2001: he is a direct witness to events. In McNeill's case, however, the NBC anchors swiftly deflect his attempts to provide a narrative of personal experience, steering him back towards what can be known and verified. Here, for example, is Frank McGee in the studio, alternately relaying McNeill's live down-the-line telephone contribution and interrogating him for further information:

> Bob informs me that he was in the motorcade. He says he was able to hear the shots. They stopped and as the shots rang out people lining the streets screamed and lay down on the sidewalk and in the street ... Bob, **have you any information** on how many times or where the President was shot? Bob **does not know** how many times or where the President was struck. **All he knows** is the President was seriously wounded and **that is the latest information** that they have.

Other interactions with McNeill similarly focus on what can be established through official sources rather than on what can be attested through a direct encounter with the event:

> Can you take it from the top, Bob, and **tell us everything that you know** if you would, please, in chronological order.

> Bob is telling me that **the latest he knows** at the moment is that the President's condition is serious and uncertain.

How might we make sense of this transformation in the relationship between the broadcaster and the people on the ground? We can note, to start with, that it is indicative of a further shift from a more indirect to a more direct form of sourcing in live breaking news stories. The analysis in this chapter of more recent catastrophe coverage has revealed not only the prevalence of experiential or attested evidentiality ('I can see ...') on the part of the anchors, but also a predilection for first-hand narratives which take as their point of departure what can be seen and heard by a co-present individual. The discussions of the 1963 material, by contrast, demonstrate both a dependence on indirect sources of evidence and a distinct disinclination to follow up on the testimony provided by direct eyewitnesses.

What kinds of explanation might we offer for this proliferation of user-generated material and eyewitness accounts in live major breaking news stories? Once again, part of the explanation must lie with the affordances of new forms of electronic media. Just as technological change is implicated in the shift from quotative to experiential evidentiality, so it has a clear role to play in the increasing availability of direct testimony. In 1963, in the absence of mobile telephony, reporters and correspondents on the scene were unable to communicate in real time with their organizations unless they could lay their hands on a landline phone or a radiophone. That these were in short supply can be demonstrated by the following anecdote, which concerns the battle in the press pool car, six cars behind the presidential limousine, for control of the means of remote real-time communication:

> As the forward part of the motorcade turned left in Dealey Plaza ... a sudden 'bam' sounded somewhere close by ... Smith counted two more cracks ... Where the bullets came from and where they went he did not know. He simply grabbed the radiophone, called the UPI Dallas bureau, and at 12:34 P.M. central standard time dictated, 'Three shots were fired at President Kennedy's motorcade today in downtown Dallas'. Throughout the world the bulletin clacked on UPI printers two minutes before the blood-spattered limousine reached Parkland Memorial Hospital. Despite rage and pummeling by Bell, his competitor from the Associated Press, Smith held the phone almost all the way to hospital. Clark of ABC, pooling for the networks, had no way to get his hands on it. It would be years before network reporters who covered the White House would be equipped with cellular phones or walkie-talkies.

(Donovan and Scherer, 1992: 59)

Nor is it only the lines of communication between media personnel and their institutions which are affected by the presence or absence of mobile technology. The rise of the citizen reporter – and the related deluge of user-generated material which has become increasingly definitional in recent breaking news coverage – is also chiefly dependent upon the large-scale availability of personal media and/or mobile transmission units. On 9/11, for instance, CNN received around two dozen amateur tapes, mostly as a consequence of people approaching their transmission trucks on the streets (Gilbert et al., 2002: 214). In 1963, by contrast, NBC did not have a mobile unit at their disposal until the morning after the assassination, as the engine of their affiliate's truck had burned out in the course of the precipitous drive to Parkland Memorial Hospital after the shooting, and arrangements had to be made to tow it around by a wrecking truck (Pettit, 1965: 63). The rapid delivery of live eyewitness accounts from the place of the event is similarly dependent upon the distribution of personal media and/or the machinery of satellite and microwave transmission. All in all, the technology which would permit the broadcasters in 2001 and 2005 to readily access people on the ground in the real time of the broadcast was either scarce or non-existent in 1963.

Such an explanation by itself, of course, will not serve to account for the way in which eyewitness testimony was marginalized by the broadcaster in 1963. NBC, as I have demonstrated, had a live link with an eyewitness in the form of their correspondent, Bob McNeill, but chose to steer him away from direct testimony and to encourage him to focus on what he had been able to glean from official sources; it also had access, via its affiliate station, to a recorded audio interview with a direct eyewitness, but it is noticeable that this interview, once played live on air, is not mentioned in the reporting that immediately follows. Other factors clearly have a role to play here in opening up the space of the eyewitness account in more recent live catastrophe coverage. We should acknowledge, inter alia, the effects of a changing media landscape (Anderson, 2004; Barkin, 2003; Ehrlich, 1997; Hamilton, 2004; Lewis et al., 2005a), in which live broadcast news providers find themselves in competition with both other channels and other media such as the internet and mobile telephony, with the consequence that there is a rush to air in which individuals on the ground become an invaluable resource in filling empty airtime, in propelling the story forward and in breaking the news fast; and we should note, too, a corresponding shift from the old-school journalism of verification towards a 'journalism of assertion', which is 'less interested in substantiating whether something is true and more interested in getting it into the public discussion' (Kovach and Rosenstiel, 1999: 8), and which can therefore warrant the use of (strictly unverifiable) personal testimony as both a source and a resource. The rise of participatory journalism can be related, furthermore, to the growth of broadcast genres such as the audience participation programme and the reality show, which are similarly centred around the delivery of 'ordinary' or 'real' people, and also to the increasing use of vox pops in news and media event broadcasting, all of which contribute to a rhetoric of authenticity across a number of non-fiction formats (Holmes, 2004; Montgomery, 2001; Van Leeuwen, 2001).

As Lewis et al. (2005b: 19) note, however, eyewitness accounts can strictly be distinguished from vox pops on the grounds that the latter involve citizens 'cast simply as citizens' (2005b: 17), individuals whose opinions are sought on the grounds that they are held to be representative of some wider constituency of the ordinary. Eyewitnesses, by contrast, stand in a privileged relationship to the event: they are extraordinary rather than ordinary, momentarily rendered unique by their proximity to history, by the simple accident of *being there*. This leads us in turn to a further factor in the growth of eyewitness accounts in live breaking news coverage: a shift over recent decades to a model of television news which is increasingly based on *presence*, on a 'fetishizing' of liveness (Winston, 2002: 15) in which immediacy becomes a significant rhetorical device. As Lewis et al. (2005a: 466) put it:

> [I]f the 'scoop' was once journalism's holy grail, the move to a 24-hour news culture has replaced it with a desire for immediacy. This is an interesting and – some might say, postmodern – turn. The classic 'scoop' is driven by investigation, the result of delving and probing. The integrity of the 'scoop' depends upon substance rather than style. The desire to be live and instantaneous shares the same instincts, but with appearance preceding substance. What matters, in the strive to be live, is presence rather than revelation. It is about covering rather than uncovering the world.

This rhetoric of presence can be related, in part at least, to the development of digital technology and to the increasing lightness and mobility of equipment: we *must* see the world because we *can*. If this appears to take the argument full circle towards a technologically-driven account once more, however, then there is more to be said.

Consider the role of correspondents-on-the-spot who are delivering a real-time commentary on the events which are unfolding around them. How might we understand the function of these individuals in the live mediation of the event? We can note, first of all, Daniel Dayan's suggestion that they are there to reinject 'the lost aura of the event':

> One wonders why these special or local correspondents are used at all, since they ... see less than their studio counterparts who monitor the output from many cameras. One might answer that their function, perhaps, is to know less, to be pressed in the crowd, elbowed, pushed around, frantically trying to perceive, see or guess ... They are there to restore the sense of distance, or specific involvement in this or that partial aspect ... By their frantic and futile attempts to see and know, they are in charge of reinjecting the lost aura of the event.

(Dayan and Katz, 2003: 96)

Such individuals, in other words, relay for the audience what it is like to be present, offering us a vicarious experience of the event and instantiating the situatedness which would be ours if we were there. Aura, as Benjamin puts it, 'is tied to ... presence' (Benjamin, 1992: 233). To reinject 'the lost aura of the event' is thus to restore a sense of presence, to offer the viewer an encounter with the unmediated event even as it is mediated for us by the broadcaster, to deliver a spasmodic but concentrated burst of *hereness* to set against the broadcasters' inevitable distanciation from the event.

The rapid recourse to eyewitness testimony which we increasingly find in live catastrophe coverage can similarly be said to be related to this question of presence. Just like the repeated exhortations to the audience to look and see for themselves which I discussed earlier in the chapter, the proliferation of eyewitness accounts contributes to the production of a rhetoric of immediacy and demediatization. Through appeals to the veridicality of the image, through the deployment of user-generated material and eyewitness accounts, television offers to presence viewers at the live event, either by positioning them as mediated observers or via the testimony of individuals who can instantiate for the audience what it would feel like to be there. As we saw in Chapter 4, the live event, at its most felicitous, transports us, sweeps us away into a moment which is unfolding in the *now* of our encounter with it. The phenomena which we have been examining in this chapter similarly work to approximate to and/or to substitute for a presence which cannot be ours if we are not actually there, but which television must work to construct in its moment-by-moment staging of the real.

7.5   Time, Space and Interactivity

As we saw in the previous section, the transformation from a more indirect to a more direct form of encounter with the breaking news event can be attributed to a number of interrelated factors. Some of these have to do with questions of affordance: television, in 1963, did not possess the technology either to communicate rapidly in real time with dispersed and mobile individuals or to deliver images live from the scene, unless the machinery of transmission had been set up in advance. Others have to do with a shift to a news ecology with a strongly competitive ethos and a corresponding dilution in those traditional journalistic values which had privileged the reliability of the source over the delivery of immediacy, and which therefore had little recourse to unverifiable testimony from individuals on the ground. Yet others have to do with discourses of authenticity and presence, which proffer the 'real', the 'genuine' and the immediate as markers of television's ability to reproduce the auratic event. If television, in other words, now offers in the early moments of live catastrophe coverage both to position us as mediated witnesses to distant events and to demediatize the event for us through the testimony of co-present individuals, then it does so because it can, and because it is driven by competitive pressures to do so, and because its own discourses of immediacy and presencing require this kind of enactment.

These new patterns of interactivity give rise, in turn, to a number of interesting phenomenological implications. In what follows I will consider two of these: the blurring of the boundaries between different participant roles in the event, and the paradox which arises from television's demediatization of the event.

We can begin to think about these questions by returning to a brief consideration of the different locales which are implicated in the delivery of the live event. As I outlined in the previous chapter, we can distinguish three significant nexi which are bound up in the event: the place in which stuff happens, the place from which television speaks the event and the place of reception. Broadcasting, typically, maintains a spatial separation between at least two of these, the place of the television event and the place of reception: hence Scannell's comment that broadcasting involves a 'doubling' of place (Scannell, 1996: 79). Each of these places, furthermore, has a characteristic set of roles associated with it: viewers, in the place of reception; presenters or performers (and in some cases a live audience), in the place from which television speaks; and participants or bystanders, in the place of the event.

As a direct consequence of the interactive transformations which I have traced in this chapter, the boundaries between these roles – and the spatial separation between the different places of the event – begin to break down. As a preliminary example of this phenomenon we can consider the anchors on the rooftops overlooking the Twin Towers on 9/11. Aaron Brown, for instance, alternates between a meditation on what he can see and hear himself as a co-present individual, and a commentary on the view of the event which he shares with the audience at home, which is visible to him on the monitor that has been set up on the roof. In doing so, he positions himself not only as a bystander but as a presenter (exhorting the audience at home to look and see for themselves) and as a viewer, locating himself at one and the same time in the place of the event (overlooking Lower Manhattan), the place from which television speaks (the rooftop) and the place of reception (watching the monitor):

And there **as you can see perhaps** the second tower, the front tower, the top portion of which is collapsing. Good Lord. There are no words, **you can see** large pieces of the building falling, **you can see** the smoking rising, **you can see** a portion the s the the the the the side of the building just being covered on the right side **as I look at it** covered in smoke, this is just a horrific scene and a horrific moment.

(CNN)

A similar collapsing of boundaries occurs in those situations where eyewitnesses make explicit reference not just to their unmediated view of the scene but also to the event as it is simultaneously playing out in a mediated form in their immediate vicinity. The CNN producer Rose Arco, for instance, was on hold, on the phone to the CNN control room and listening to CNN radio when she saw from the window of the apartment a man jumping from one of the towers (Gilbert et al., 2002: 49); like Brown on the rooftop she was thus simultaneously accessing the event in a mediated form (via the radio), contributing to the narrative construction of the event (on the phone) and viewing it as a direct eyewitness. And here is a member of the public, live on CBS, who is again both audience and co-present bystander at one and the same moment:

> At that point all the news media started to learn about it and **I turned on my radio**, and while I was sitting at my desk I **saw** a second jet, fairly large plane, fly in over the south end of Manhattan and deliberately flying directly into the Trade Center **before my eyes**.

(CBS)

Or consider the case of the airline passengers on a plane which was preparing for an emergency landing in Los Angeles in September 2005. Many of them were watching cable news channels which were covering their situation live on air, thus simultaneously positioning themselves as participants and as viewers. As one passenger would comment later to the *LA Times*, 'My friend said: Hey dude, something's wrong with our plane. We're on TV' (*The Guardian*, 23 September 2005).

These kinds of examples clearly demonstrate the way in which both the increasingly complex connectivity of the event and the heightened mobility of electronic forms of communication have come to blur the line between participant and viewer, between anchor and eyewitness. The 1963 NBC broadcast maintained a clear distinction between the roles of individuals caught up in the event: the anchors in the studio who were there to relay the news to the audience at home, and who were unable to experience what was transpiring in either a mediated or an unmediated form; the correspondent-on-the-spot whose responsibility was information gathering, and who had limited licence to reproduce a narrative of personal experience based on what he had seen and heard in person. A parallel separation was maintained between the different places that were implicated in the event: the locales in which stuff was happening (Dealey Plaza; the Dallas Trade Mart; the Dallas Memorial Hospital; Washington), the places from which the event was spoken (the NBC studio and the studios of its affiliate in Dallas), and the places of reception (the terminal points, from which one could view television's delivery of the event but could not speak it). In the case of 9/11 and subsequent live catastrophe coverage, by contrast, members of the public and professionals may come to contribute to the discursive formation of the event even as they witness what is going on as co-present individuals and/or consume it via live media.

One significant consequence of this blurring of boundaries is what we might refer to as the *paradox of demediatization*. The coverage of the Menezes shooting in 2005 will serve as an excellent example of what I have in mind here. Consider, for example, the live eyewitness testimony concerning Menezes' behaviour at Stockwell Station. One eyewitness saw a man vaulting over the ticket barriers and running down into the underground, followed by a number of police officers. Another eyewitness saw men running on to the train. Based on the developing story, the eyewitnesses assumed that the first man was Menezes, and thus described the behaviour of the individuals they had seen in terms of a notion of *pursuit*:

> I was sitting on the uh uh tube train, it hadn't pulled out of the station at this time but the doors were still open. I heard um a lot of shouting, get down, get out. I looked to my right, I saw a chap run onto the onto the train um Asian guy um he ran onto the train sort of [—] he was running so fast he half sort of tripped but he was being **pursued** by three guys, one had a black handgun in his hand, left hand, uh as he sort of went down two of them sort of dropped onto him to hold him down and the other one fired the gun, I heard five shots … I was maybe four or five yards along where this accident happened, I I watched it.

This notion, widespread in the eyewitness testimony, was in turn taken up and treated as a given by BBC News 24 in their coverage:

> From the eyewitnesses you've spoken to, is it clear **why the police were pursuing this man into the train**?

> … there is a lot of speculation, people here suggesting that this man had been **pursued**, followed, they knew what they were dealing with and they had challenged him, although I must say no-one heard such a challenge, and therefore he was shot.

> So just to recap on the events of the last hour and a half, we're through eyewitness accounts getting piecing together a picture of what happened at Stockwell this morning, just after 10 o'clock. All those eyewitnesses say that a man ran jumped the barriers at Stockwell tube station, ran onto the Northern Line station, onto the train, hotly **pursued** by plain clothes officers who shot five times into his body at close range and killed him. Mayhem then ensued, mayhem and panic the words which come up repeatedly again and again of the response from the people on the platform and on the train at Stockwell.

> There were two key eyewitnesses that we spoke to very early after just arriving here … uh one man said he was in the in the uh the main concourse of the rather small station here and he saw a man run past him, now he said he couldn't um describe him uh but he ran past, this man, then vaulted over the ticket barriers … and then ran down into the uh into the bowels of the station and the man was **pursued** by several armed police officers according to this eyewitness uh who uh who then **chased** him into the station and the eyewitness said he heard several bangs a bit like a shot gun before he then ran off out of the station, the eyewitness that is.

It rapidly became clear in the aftermath of the event that this was not an accurate account. As the BBC's website would later put it: 'CCTV footage is said to show the man walking at normal pace into the station, picking up a copy of a free news-paper and apparently passing through the barriers before descending the escalator to the platform and running to a train. He boarded a Tube train, paused, looking left and right, and sat in a seat facing the platform'. One eyewitness later told a newspaper that the man vaulting the barrier must have been a police officer.[4]

BBC News 24 was by no means alone in its generation of an inaccurate and misleading account of what had happened at Stockwell. Menezes was shot, according to eyewitnesses, because he was wearing a thick coat, which was odd on a hot day in July; furthermore he was running away from the police. He was Asian; possibly Pakistani; there was a smoking package and a strong chemical smell in the air at Stockwell Station; according to one account he 'appeared to be wearing a "bomb belt with wires coming out"';[5] he was shot five times. None of this, it turned out, was correct. Menezes, according to a member of the police surveillance team and also the CCTV footage, was wearing a blue denim jacket and not a thick coat; there was no bomb belt, and no wires. He was not Asian, let alone Pakistani, but Brazilian. There was no smoking package and no smoke. Nor was he shot five times: the post-mortem examination showed that he had been shot seven times in the head, and once in the shoulder, and that a further three bullets had missed him.

It is here that the paradox of demediatization enters the picture. As I suggested in the previous section, we can make sense of television's increasing reliance on eyewitness testimony in terms of a staging of the real, a demediatization of the event in the course of which co-present individuals come to instantiate for the remote audience what it is like to be there. The testimony of the eyewitness, furthermore, is typically accorded a more authoritative status than the accounts of others whose knowledge is acquired at a remove. Peters (2001: 715) cites Locke here, who argues that the credibility of testimony diminishes in proportion to its distance from the 'original truth':

> A credible man vouching his knowledge of it is a good proof; but if another, equally credible, do witness it from his report, the testimony is weaker; and a third, that attests the hearsay of a hearsay, is yet less considerable. So that *in traditional truths, each remove weakens the force of the proof*; and the more hands the tradition has successively passed through, the less strength and evidence it receives from them.

(Locke, 1964: 258, cited in Peters, 2001: 715, original emphasis)

Eyewitnesses, however, are not conduits through which the event speaks itself; they are individuals who mediate the event as they speak it, and whose mediation of the event imposes a structure of interpretation upon the material which they enunciate. Their testimony is, furthermore, notoriously unreliable (Allport and Postman, 1948: 54). As Peters himself goes on to argue, every act of testimony is thus at the same time an act of mediation:

> A private experience enables a public statement. But the journey from experience (the seen) into the world (the said) is precarious … No transfusion of consciousness is possible. Words can be exchanged, experiences cannot.

(Peters, 2001: 710)

---

[4]http://news.bbc.co.uk/1/hi/uk/4158832.stm (accessed 1 September 2005).
[5]http://news.bbc.co.uk/1/hi/uk/4706787.stm (accessed 1 September 2005).

The attempt to demediatize the event through the delivery of first-hand testimony from those who were there can thus paradoxically lead to a conflict between competing mediations of the event. This becomes clear from a further examination of the BBC News 24 material. As Kovach and Rosenstiel (2001) write, much of the work of journalists now has less to do with controlling the rate at which information can be released and more to do with 'helping audiences make sense of it'. The following examples demonstrate just this process at work, as the BBC News 24 anchor attempts to make sense of competing eyewitness accounts of the event by requesting clarification from a correspondent-on-the-spot and then from a security expert in the studio:

> Andy, make some sense of all this, can you, can you piece it together. I mean we had a graphic eyewitness account of a man who saw another man being shot dead by police, **we've heard from other passengers** on a different train of a smoking package in a carriage?

> Gordon it's all very mystifying, isn't it, what happened and why it it seems as if there were two incidents at Stockwell Station. **We've just heard** very graphically of how police pursued a man onto the carriage and shot him dead but **we heard earlier from other eyewitnesses** on a different train talking about smoking coming from a carriage. **Other passengers said** they saw a package apparently smoking there was a very strange industrial smell.

In their attempts to make sense of competing mediations of the event, the anchors even attempt to recruit the eyewitnesses themselves as arbitrators. Not surprisingly, this causes a certain amount of confusion:

Anchor   Now that you've heard a few more details about what's happened there about Scotland Yard confirming that they shot dead a man, does anything that you saw, does it fit into any pattern you can recognize?

E/w   um um in in in what way, I'm sorry, I'm not sure I understand what you're asking.

Anchor   Well sin since you were there clearly you weren't directly involved in seeing anybody suspicious or any uh smoking packages or anything like that but now that you know that a man was shot dead uh one one of those tube trains and we've heard from other eyewitnesses of on other train that there was smoke coming from it duh does it make any sense to you?

E/w   Well yeah I mean obviously um [—] the train that I was on was receiving people from the opposite platform who had directly witnessed an incident and they were very very visibly shaken, they'd obviously seen somebody um they'd seen [—] police police they'd seen something occurred so yeah it completely ties in with that um but like I said I didn't actually see anything myself in directly related to the shooting I just saw the ensuing panic and the kind of aftermath of it, if you like.

The paradoxical consequences of demediatization and eyewitness testimony are by no means limited to this one event. As a further and useful example we can return to a brief consideration of the live catastrophe coverage on 9/11. The following, from CNN, will suffice to provide a flavour of what I have in mind here:

E/w   I just heard another very loud bang and a very large plane that might have been a DC9 or a 747 flew past my window and I think it may have hit the Trade Center.

Anchor To be honest, Elliot, I didn't get I didn't get the impression that it was that big a plane.

Here the proliferation of eyewitness testimony and the blurring of the boundaries between participant roles have together led to a conflict between competing mediations of the event, as the anchor, a mediated witness to the second plane impact, enters into a disagreement with an eyewitness over the precise details of what has happened, as viewed from their respective vantage points.

7.6   Absence, Presence and the Live Television Event

This is one of many scenarios that will take place in the future. The ability to know first hand how your partner or partners are responding while having sex. Not a week later, if at all, but in the moment. Not to mention that your partners are not in bed with you, but in different locations across the planet. You are actually experiencing euphoria via simulated telepresence sex with teletactile experiences.[6]

In a 1992 paper on virtual reality, Steuer discusses the extent to which mediated encounters can deliver a sense of being there, of being present in a remote environment. Following Minsky (1980), Steuer uses the term *telepresence* to examine this issue:

When perception is mediated by a communication technology, one is forced to perceive two separate environments simultaneously: the physical environment in which one is actually present and the environment presented by the medium. The term telepresence can be used to describe the precedence of the latter experience in favour of the former; that is, telepresence is the extent to which one feels present in the mediated environment, rather than in the immediate physical environment.

(Steuer, 1992: 75)

Steuer's view is that an individual's sensation of telepresence varies in relation to two parameters, which he refers to as *vividness* and *interactivity*. The first of these has to do with the number of senses a communicative channel engages simultaneously. Interactivity, by contrast, is related to the extent to which we have the power to influence either the form or the content of the mediated environment (Steuer, 1992: 80).

A strong feeling of being there, on this account, would require both that a number of our senses are engaged with the remote locale and that we are able to act upon it in the real time of the encounter. If we return briefly to Evans' discussion of the remotely controlled submarine which we examined in Chapter 1,

---

[6]http://www.natasha.cc/sex.htm (accessed 8 August 2006).

for example, then we can rank that experience as relatively highly interactive (insofar as the individual 'in the bowels of a ship' can pick up objects on the seabed); at the same time, it will be relatively low on the vividness continuum, if we assume that the operator has some way of seeing the objects that he is physically manipulating, but cannot smell, touch, taste or hear them. Something closer to a true virtual reality experience, such as the 'full teletactile bodysuit in which touch, impact will involve the whole body' which Virilio imagines in his dystopic study *Open Sky* (Virilio, 1995: 39), on the other hand, would seem to deliver a greater degree of vividness as well as preserving the interactivity of Evans' original case. In Steuer's schema, the 'teletactile bodysuit' would thus be regarded as delivering a high degree of telepresence, a strong sense of being there: in the terms that I outlined in Chapter 1 it would appear to be a relatively thick encounter, allowing the individual to see, hear and touch the remote environment.

Television, as I argued at the beginning of this book, is unable to deliver a thick encounter with the event. Just like Evans' submarine example, it is low on the vividness continuum; and whilst some live television genres provide a level of interactivity via the use of mobile phones and texting, their ability to deliver a feeling of control over the remote environment is limited to what can be achieved through verbal means alone: eliciting chat from a television presenter, entering a real-time competition, buying goods, inducing a performer on a soft-porn channel to wiggle or uncover a particular part of her anatomy.

In the conclusion to Chapter 1, I suggested that mediated interactions might possess a set of mechanisms to compensate for the thinness of this encounter between the viewer and the television event. I argued, furthermore, that they needed to be considered not simply in terms of their inadequacies when compared to canonical encounters but also in terms of the advantages and gratifications which they offer as a consequence of their ability to permit encounters at a distance.

This book is by no means the first work to cover this territory. Research over the last decades has suggested, for example, that 'para-social interactions' – encounters in which the remote viewer is given 'an illusion of face-to-face relationship with the performer' (Horton and Wohl, 1986: 185) – are an important element in mediated communication. The para-social phenomenon of direct address to the audience has been discussed in relation to a number of non-fiction broadcast phenomena such as radio DJ talk (Montgomery, 1986), television chat shows (Tolson, 1985), documentaries (Corner, 1991), daytime magazine programmes (Moores, 1995), sports presenting (Whannel, 1992), newscasting, and television advertising (Corner, 1995; Ellis, 1992). The simulation of 'expressive eye contact' with the viewer (Corner, 1991: 32) via direct gaze to camera has also been discussed, as have a variety of linguistic markers such as colloquial speech rhythms (Corner, 1991), the occurrence of 'back-stage speech' (Moores, 1995) and the use of expressions such as *nowadays* as a 'reiterated assertion of a co-temporality' (Brunsdon and Morley, 1978: 19).

What is at stake in all of these instances is the use of an interpersonal mode which has the effect, to a greater or lesser extent, of re-situating performer and audience within an interactional context which approximates to the norms of the canonical encounter. As Scannell puts it (1991: 2):

> [W]hile the central fact of broadcasting's communicative context is that it speaks from one place and is heard in another, the design of talk on radio and TV recognises this and attempts to bridge the gap by simulating co-presence with its listeners and viewers.

In this chapter I have examined further aspects of the way in which television – and live television in particular – works to presence its audience. The comparison between the broadcasts in the immediate aftermath of the Kennedy assassination in 1963 and turn-of-the-century coverage of breaking news stories such as 9/11, 7/7 and the Menezes shooting has provided evidence of a shift from a more indirect to a more direct relation to the event. In the preceding sections I have described this transformation with particular reference to a growing emphasis on the moment of witness, and I have suggested that we can examine this phenomenon both in terms of the ability of presenters and audience to view what is happening in the moment of its unfolding, and in terms of the proliferation of live testimony from the place of the event. I have gone on to trace some interesting implications of this shift: the blurring or collapsing of boundaries between different participant roles and different places, and the multiple and conflicting mediations of the event which paradoxically come into being as a consequence of television's attempts to demediatize the event by presencing the viewer. I have suggested, as well, a number of interrelated explanations for this continuing shift into a mode of presence-in-absence in live breaking news coverage: the pressures of a competitive news marketplace; the increasing availability of personal media and other forms of mobile communication-at-a-distance; a shift in the direction of a discourse of authenticity and the 'real' across many non-fictional television genres; and a powerful rhetoric of presence and immediacy which has come, as a consequence of these other transformations, to be a significant factor in the delivery of the live event.

If this notion of the presencing of the viewer permits us to inspect the kind of work which television must do to compensate for its inevitable distanciation from the event, however, then it also allows us to reflect upon the advantages which complex connectivity delivers for encounters between remote individuals.

In Chapter 2 of this book we examined the notion of the simultaneity of elsewheres to which the individual has access through the real-time interactions afforded by electronic forms of communication. When the *New York Times*, in the aftermath of the *Titanic* disaster in 1912, commented with some wonder on the 'almost magic use of the air' to send messages speeding from one remote place to another it seems unlikely that the writer could have imagined the extraordinary communicative complexity which would ensue within a century. At any given moment, day or night, innumerable messages ricochet from one point to another, carried near-instantaneously between remote sites by media both wireless and wired. Pagers beep; phones ring; fax machines announce the imminent arrival of a new document; a sound on a computer indicates that a new email has arrived; a voice on the radio informs the listener about local weather conditions or rain hundreds of miles away or storm-force winds on another continent; on the television a correspondent clutches a railing, nearly bowled over by the wind and drenched by sea spray as he delivers a live report from the site of an incoming hurricane to a viewer on the other side of the world. To seize upon some individual instant and attempt to map these communication flows in the manner of a time-and-motion expert charting the movements of individuals around a workplace would be an impossible endeavour: the world is thick with messages, invisibly crossing and re-crossing each other in apparently endless and interlinked circuits of interaction.

If we wish to preserve, in such a world, the kind of clear distinction between face-to-face and mediated encounters with which this book began, then we must take account not only of the extent to which the electronic media 'bring the world' into individual contexts of co-presence but also of the way in which they permit us to actively engage with a multiplicity of simultaneous elsewheres in which a cacophony of voices are speaking the event. It is, of course, still the case that it is the broadcaster who institutionally enunciates the event, with user-generated material and eyewitness accounts embedded and contextualized within the overarching narrative framework which television generates in the real time of transmission and reception. Developments in online participatory journalism and 'we media' (Bowman and Willis, 2003; Gillmor, 2004), however, make it clear that there are other models in circulation in which the distinctions between producer and receiver, mediated and direct witness, an institution and its publics, *here* and *there* continue to be eroded.

References

Adam, B. 1990. *Time and Social Theory*. Cambridge: Polity Press.

Allan, S. 2002. 'Reweaving the Internet: Online News of September 11'. In B. Zelizer and S. Allan (eds.), *Journalism after September 11*. London: Routledge, pp. 119–140.

Allport, G. and L. Postman. 1948. *The Psychology of Rumor*. New York: Henry Holt.

Anderson, B.M. 2004. *News Flash: Journalism, Infotainment and the Bottom-line Business of Broadcast News*. San Francisco: Jossey-Bass.

Anderson, L.B. 1986. 'Evidentials, Paths of Change, and Mental Maps: Typologically Regular Asymmetries'. In W. Chafe and J. Nichols (eds.), *Evidentiality: The Linguistic Coding of Epistemology*. Norwood, NJ: Ablex Publishing Corporation, pp. 273–312.

Atkinson, R.M. and P.D. Griffiths. 1973. 'Here's Here's, There's, Here and There'. *Edinburgh Working Papers in Linguistics*, pp. 29–73.

Austin, J.L. 2005. *How to Do Things with Words*. Cambridge, MA: Harvard University Press.

Avery, R.K. and T.A. McCain. 1986. 'Interpersonal and Mediated Encounters: A Reorientation to the Mass Communication Process'. In G. Gumpert and R. Cathcart (eds.), *Inter/Media: Interpersonal Communication in a Media World*. New York: Oxford University Press, pp. 121–131.

Barkin, S.M. 2003. *American Television News: The Media Marketplace and the Public Interest*. New York: M. E. Sharpe Inc.

Benjamin, W. 1973. *Charles Baudelaire: A Lyric Poet in the Era of High Capitalism*. London: New Left Books.

Benjamin, W. 1992. 'The Work of Art in the Age of Mechanical Production'. In W. Benjamin, *Illuminations*. London: Fontana Press, pp. 211–244.

Benveniste, E. 1971. *Problems in General Linguistics*. Coral Gables, FL: University of Miami Press.

Bergson, H. 1911. *Creative Evolution*. London: Macmillan.

Bergson, H. 1988. *Matter and Memory*. New York: Zone.

Bourdon, J. 2000. 'Live Television is Still Alive: On Television as an Unfulfilled Promise'. *Media, Culture and Society* 22, pp. 531–556.

Bowman, S. and C. Willis. 2003. *We Media: How Audiences are Shaping the Future of News and Information*. www.hypergene.net/wemedia/

Brunn, S.D. and T.R. Leinbach. 1991. 'Introduction'. In S.D. Brunn and T.R. Leinbach (eds.), *Collapsing Space and Time: Geographic Aspects of Communication and Information*. London: HarperCollins, pp. xv–xxvi.

Brunsdon, C. and D. Morley. 1978. *Everyday Television: Nationwide*. London: British Film Institute.

Bühler, K. 1982. 'The Deictic Field of Language and Deictic Words'. In R.J. Jarvella and W. Klein (eds.), *Speech, Place and Action*. New York: Wiley, pp. 9–30.

Bybee, J. 1985. *Morphology: A Study of the Relation between Meaning and Form*. Amsterdam: John Benjamins.

Caldwell, J.T. 1995. *Televisuality: Style, Crisis, and Authority in American Television*. New Brunswick, NJ: Rutgers University Press.

Carey, J.W. 1989. *Communication as Culture: Essays on Media and Society*. London: Unwin Hyman.

Carey, J.W. 2002. 'American Journalism on, before and after September 11'. In B. Zelizer and S. Allan (eds.), *Journalism after September 11*. London: Routledge, pp. 71–90.

Cathcart, B. 1997. *Were You Still Up for Portillo?* Harmondsworth: Penguin.

Chafe, W. 1986. 'Evidentiality in English Conversation and Academic Writing'. In W. Chafe and J. Nichols (eds.), *Evidentiality: The Linguistic Coding of Epistemology*. Norwood, NJ: Ablex Publishing Corporation, pp. 261–272.

Chung, S. and A. Timberlake. 1985. 'Tense, Aspect, and Mood'. In T. Shopen (ed.), *Language Typology and Syntactic Description: Grammatical Categories and the Lexicon*. Volume 3. Cambridge: Cambridge University Press, pp. 202–258.

Corner, J. 1991. 'The Interview as Social Encounter'. In P. Scannell (ed.), *Broadcast Talk*. London: Sage, pp. 31–47.

Corner, J. 1995. *Television Form and Public Address*. London: Edward Arnold.

Day, J. 2005. 'We Had 50 Images within an Hour'. *Media Guardian* 11 July, p. 2.

Dayan, D. and E. Katz. 2003. *Media Events: Live Broadcasting of History*. Cambridge, MA: Harvard University Press.

DeClerk, R. 1991. *Tense in English: Its Structure and Use in Discourse*. London: Routledge.

Doane, M.A. 1990. 'Information, Crisis, Catastrophe'. In P. Mellencamp (ed.), *Logics of Television*. Bloomington, IN: Indiana University Press, pp. 222–239.

Donovan, R.J. and R. Scherer. 1992. *Unsilent Revolution: Television News and American Public Life*. New York: Cambridge University Press.

Ehrlich, M.C. 1997. 'The Competitive Ethos in Television Newswork'. In D. Berkowitz (ed.), *Social Meanings of News*. Thousand Oaks, CA: Sage, pp. 301–317.

Ellis, J. 1992. *Visible Fictions: Cinema, Television, Video*. 2nd edn. London: Routledge.

Ellis, J. 2000. *Seeing Things: Television in the Age of Uncertainty*. London: I.B. Tauris.

Evans, G. 1982. *The Varieties of Reference*. Oxford: Clarendon Press.

Ferguson, M. 1990. 'Electronic Media and the Redefining of Time and Space'. In M. Ferguson (ed.), *Public Communication: The New Imperatives*. London: Sage, pp. 152–172.

Feuer, J. 1983. 'The Concept of Live Television: Ontology as Ideology'. In E.A. Kaplan (ed.), *Regarding Television: Critical Approaches*. Los Angeles: American Film Institute, pp. 12–21.

Fillmore, C.J. 1975. *Santa Cruz Lectures on Deixis*. Mimeo, Indiana University Linguistics Club.

Fillmore, C.J. 1982. 'Towards a Descriptive Framework for Spatial Deixis'. In R.J. Jarvella and W. Klein (eds.), *Speech, Place and Action*. New York: Wiley, pp. 31–59.

Fixter, A. 2005. 'London. 9.11 am: Liverpool Street Has Been Closed after a "Bang"'. *Press Gazette* 15 July, p. 18.

Gale, R.M. 1968. *The Language of Time*. London: Routledge and Kegan Paul.

Genette, G. 1980. *Narrative Discourse: An Essay in Method*. Ithaca, NY: Cornell University Press.

Gibson, J.J. 1982. *Reasons for Realism: Selected Essays*. Hillsdale, NJ: Lawrence Erlbaum Associates.

Giddens, A. 1990. *The Consequences of Modernity*. Cambridge: Polity Press.

Gilbert, A., P. Hirschkorn, M. Murphy, R. Walensky and M. Stephens. 2002. *Covering Catastrophe: Broadcast Journalists Report September 11*. Chicago: Bonus Books.

Gillmor, D. 2004. *We the Media: Grassroots Journalism by the People, for the People*. Sebastopol, CA: O'Reilly.

Goffman, E. 1978. *The Presentation of Self in Everyday Life*. Harmondsworth: Penguin.

Goffman, E. 1981. *Forms of Talk*. Philadelphia: University of Pennsylvania Press.

Gould, P. 1991. 'Dynamic Structures of Geographic Space'. In S.D. Brunn and T.R. Leinbach (eds.), *Collapsing Space and Time: Geographic Aspects of Communication and Information*. London: HarperCollins, pp. 3–30.

Grice, H.P. 1975. 'Logic and Conversation'. In P. Cole and J.L. Morgan (eds.), *Syntax and Semantics 3: Speech Acts*. New York: Academic Press, pp. 41–58.

Grint, K. and S. Woolgar. 1997. *The Machine at Work*. Cambridge: Polity Press.

Hallin, D.C. 1993. *We Keep America on Top of the World: Television Journalism and the Public Sphere*. London: Routledge.

Hamilton, J.T. 2004. *All the News that's Fit to Sell: How the Market Transforms Information into News*. Princeton, NJ: Princeton University Press.

Hammond, M., J. Howarth and R. Keat. 1991. *Understanding Phenomenology*. Oxford: Basil Blackwell.

Harvey, D. 1990. *The Condition of Postmodernity*. Oxford: Blackwell.

Heath, S. and G. Skirrow. 1977. 'Television: A World in Action'. *Screen* 18(2), pp. 7–59.

Heritage, J. 1984. *Garfinkel and Ethnomethodology*. Cambridge: Polity Press.

Heritage, J. 1985. 'Analyzing News Interviews: Aspects of the Production of Talk for an Overhearing Audience'. In T.A. van Dijk (ed.), *Handbook of Discourse Analysis*. London: Academic Press, pp. 95–117.

Heritage, J. and D. Greatbatch. 1991. 'On the Institutional Character of Institutional Talk: The Case of News Interviews'. In D. Boden and D.H. Zimmerman (eds.), *Talk and Social Structure*. Cambridge: Polity Press, pp. 93–137.

Hjarvard, S. 1994. 'TV News: From Discrete Items to Continuous Narrative? The Social Meaning of Changing Temporal Structures'. *Cultural Studies* 8(2), pp. 306–320.

Holmes, S. 2004. 'But This Time You Choose!: Approaching the Interactive Audience of Reality TV'. *International Journal of Cultural Studies* 7(2), pp. 213–231.

Horton, D. and R.R. Wohl. 1986. 'Mass Communication and Para-Social Interaction: Observation on Intimacy at a Distance'. In G. Gumpert and R. Cathcart (eds.), *Inter/Media: Interpersonal Communication in a Media World*. New York: Oxford University Press, pp. 185–206.

Houston, B. 1984. 'Viewing Television: The Metapsychology of Endless Consumption'. *Quarterly Review of Film Studies* 9(3), pp. 183–195.

Hu, V. 2001. 'Americans Turn to Web Sites to Post Information, Reactions'. *Sfgate.com* 12 September.

Husserl, E. 1964. *The Phenomenology of Internal Time-Consciousness*. Bloomington, IN: Indiana University Press.

Husserl, E. 1970 [1936]. *The Crisis of European Sciences and Transcendental Phenomenology*. Evanston, IL: Northwestern University Press.

Hutchby, I. 2001. *Conversation and Technology*. Cambridge: Polity Press.

Innis, H.A. 1951. *The Bias of Communication*. Toronto: University of Toronto Press.

Janelle, D.G. 1968. 'Central Place Development in a Time-Space Framework'. *The Professional Geographer* XX, pp. 5–10.

Janelle, D.G. 1973. 'Measuring Human Extensibility in a Shrinking World'. *The Journal of Geography* 72(5), pp. 8–15.

Janelle, D.G. 1991. 'Global Interdependence and its Consequences'. In S.D. Brunn and T.R. Leinbach (eds.), *Collapsing Space and Time: Geographic Aspects of Communication and Information*. London: HarperCollins, pp. 49–81.

Kern, S. 1983. *The Culture of Time and Space, 1880–1918*. Cambridge, MA: Harvard University Press.

Klein, W. 1994. *Time in Language*. London: Routledge.

Kovach, B. and T. Rosenstiel. 1999. *Warp Speed: America in the Age of Mixed Media*. New York: The Century Foundation Press.

Kovach, B. and T. Rosenstiel. 2001. *The Elements of Journalism: What Newspeople Should Know and the Public Should Expect*. New York: Crown.

Lagan, S. 2005. 'Londoners Turn to *Standard* as Horror of Attacks Unfolds'. *Press Gazette* 15 July, p. 17.

Levinson, S. 1983. *Pragmatics*. Cambridge: Cambridge University Press.

Lewis, J., S. Cushion and J. Thomas. 2005a. 'Immediacy, Convenience or Engagement? An Analysis of 24-Hour News Channels in the UK'. *Journalism Studies* 6(4), pp. 461–477.

Lewis, J., S. Inthorn and K. Wahl-Jorgensen. 2005b. *Citizens or Consumers: What the Media Tell Us about Political Participation*. Maidenhead: Open University Press.

Love, R.L. 1965. 'The Business of Television and the Black Weekend'. In B.S. Greenberg and E.B. Parker (eds.), *The Kennedy Assassination and the American Public*. Stanford, CA: Stanford University Press, pp. 73–86.

Lyons, J. 1977. *Semantics*. Cambridge: Cambridge University Press.

Lyons, J. 1982. 'Deixis and Subjectivity: Loquor, Ergo Sum?' In R.J. Jarvella and W. Klein (eds.), *Speech, Place and Action*. New York: Wiley, pp. 101–124.

McAnally, M., A.B. Wilson and C. Norris. 1993. 'What Drives Live? Why Broadcasters Choose to Transmit Live Programming'. In N. Miller and R. Allen (eds.), *It's Live – But is it Real?* London: John Libbey, pp. 15–21.

McLuhan, M. 1973. *Understanding Media*. London: Abacus.

McTaggart, J.M.E. 1927. *The Nature of Existence*. Volume II. London: Cambridge University Press.

Marriott, S. 1995. 'Intersubjectivity and Temporal Reference in Television Commentary'. *Time and Society* 4(3), pp. 345–364.

Marriott, S. 1996. 'Time and Time Again: "Live" Television Commentary and the Construction of Replay Talk'. *Media, Culture and Society* 18, pp. 69–86.

Marriott, S. 1997. 'The Emergence of Live Television Talk'. *Text* 17(2), pp. 181–198.

Marriott, S. 2000. 'Election Night'. *Media, Culture and Society* 22, pp. 131–148.

Marriott, S. 2001. 'In Pursuit of the Ineffable: How Television Found the Eclipse but Lost the Plot'. *Media, Culture and Society* 23, pp. 725–742.

Marriott, S. 2007. 'American Election Night and the Journalism of Assertion'. *Journalism: Theory, Practice and Criticism* 8(6), in press.

Massey, D. 1993. 'Power-Geometry and a Progressive Sense of Place'. In J. Bird, B. Curtis, T. Putnam, G. Robertson and L. Tickner (eds.), *Mapping the Futures: Local Cultures, Global Change*. London: Routledge, pp. 59–69.

Mellencamp, P. 1990. 'TV Time and Catastrophe'. In P. Mellencamp (ed.), *Logics of Television*. Bloomington, IN: Indiana University Press, pp. 240–266.

Merleau-Ponty, M. 1962. *Phenomenology of Perception*. London: Routledge.

Metz, C. 1974. *Film Language: A Semiotics of the Cinema*. New York: Oxford University Press.

Meyrowitz, J. 1986. 'Television and Interpersonal Behavior: Codes of Perception and Response'. In G. Gumpert and R. Cathcart (eds.), *Inter/Media: Interpersonal Communication in a Media World*. New York: Oxford University Press, pp. 253–272.

Miller, G.A. and P.N. Johnson-Laird. 1976. *Language and Perception*. Cambridge: Cambridge University Press.

Minsky, M. 1980. 'Telepresence'. *Omni* 2, pp. 44–52.

Montgomery, M. 1986. 'DJ Talk'. *Media, Culture and Society* 8(4), pp. 421–440.

Montgomery, M. 2001. 'Defining Authentic Talk'. *Discourse Studies* 3(4), pp. 397–405.

Montgomery, M. 2006. 'Broadcast News, the Live "Two-Way" and the Case of Andrew Gilligan'. *Media, Culture and Society* 28(2): 233–259.

Moores, S. 1995. 'TV Discourse and "Time-Space Distanciation": On Mediated Interaction in Modern Society'. *Time and Society* 4(3), pp. 329–344.

Moores, S. 1997. 'Broadcasting and its Audiences'. In H. Mackay (ed.), *Consumption and Everyday Life*. London: Sage, pp. 213–246.

Morris, B.S. and J. Nydahl. 1985. 'Sport Spectacle as Drama'. *Journal of Popular Culture* 18(4), pp. 101–110.

Morse, M. 1983. 'Sport on Television: Replay and Display'. In A. Kaplan (ed.), *Regarding Television: Critical Approaches*. Los Angeles: American Film Institute, pp. 44–66.

Morse, M. 1985. 'Talk, Talk, Talk: The Space of Discourse on Television'. *Screen* 26(2), pp. 2–17.

Nimmo, D. and J.E. Combs. 1985. *Nightly Horrors: Crisis Coverage in Television Network News*. Knoxville, TN: University of Tennessee Press.

Nowotny, H. 1994. *Time: The Modern and Postmodern Experience*. Cambridge: Polity Press.

Ong, W. 1977. *Interfaces of the Word: Studies in the Evolution of Consciousness and Culture*. London: Cornell University Press.

Peters, J.D. 1999. *Speaking into the Air: A History of the Idea of Communication*. Chicago: The University of Chicago Press.

Peters, J.D. 2001. 'Witnessing'. *Media, Culture and Society* 23, pp. 707–723.

Pettit, T. 1965. 'The Television Story in Dallas'. In B.S. Greenberg and E.B. Parker (eds.), *The Kennedy Assassination and the American Public*. Stanford, CA: Stanford University Press, pp. 61–66.

Pike, C. 2005. 'From Power Surge to Bombs – How TV Broke the News'. *Press Gazette* 15 July, p. 18.

Reeves, I. 2005. 'Mobloggers Show They Are a Force in Newsgathering'. *Press Gazette* 15 July, p. 17.

Rommetveit, R. 1968. *Words, Meaning and Messages*. London: Academic Press.

Rommetveit, R. 1973. *On Message Structure*. New York: Wiley.

Ryan, P. 1974. *Cybernetics of the Sacred*. New York: Anchor Press.

Scannell, P. 1991. 'Introduction: The Relevance of Talk'. In P. Scannell (ed.), *Broadcast Talk*. London: Sage, pp. 1–13.

Scannell, P. 1996. *Radio, Television and Modern Life*. Oxford: Blackwell.

Scannell, P. 1999. 'The Death of Diana and the Meaning of Media Events'. *Review of Media, Information and Society* 4, pp. 27–50.

Scannell, P. 2000. 'For-Anyone-As-Someone Structures'. *Media, Culture and Society* 22(1), pp. 5–24.

Schramm, W. 1965. 'Communication in Crisis'. In B.S. Greenberg and E.B. Parker (eds.), *The Kennedy Assassination and the American Public*. Stanford, CA: Stanford University Press, pp. 1–25.

Schutz, A. 1962. *Collected Papers*. Volume I. The Hague, Netherlands: M. Nijhoff.

Schutz, A. 1970. *Reflections on the Problem of Relevance*. New Haven and London: Yale University Press.

Schutz, A. 1972. *The Phenomenology of the Social World*. London: Heinemann.

Schutz, A. and T. Luckmann. 1983. *The Structures of the Life-World*. Volume II. Evanston, IL: Northwestern University Press.

Steuer, J. 1992. 'Defining Virtual Reality: Dimensions Determining Telepresence'. *Journal of Communication* 42(4), pp. 73–93.

Stevenson, N. 1995. *Understanding Media Cultures: Social Theory and Mass Communication*. London: Sage.

Thompson, J.B. 1995. *The Media and Modernity: A Social Theory of the Media*. Cambridge: Polity Press.

Tolson, A. 1985. 'Anecdotal Television'. *Screen* 26(2), pp. 18–27.

Tolson, A. 1996. *Mediations: Text and Discourse in Media Studies*. London: Hodder Arnold.

Tomlinson, J. 1999. *Globalization and Culture*. Cambridge: Polity Press.

Turner, V. 1969. *The Ritual Process: Structure and Anti-Structure*. Ithaca, NY: Cornell University Press.

Van Leeuwen, T. 2001. 'What is Authenticity?' *Discourse Studies* 3(4), pp. 392–397.

Vendler, Z. 1967. *Linguistics in Philosophy*. Ithaca, NY: Cornell University Press.

Vianello, R. 1985. 'The Power Politics of "Live" Television'. *Journal of Film and Video* 37, pp. 26–40.

Virilio, P. 1991. *Lost Dimension*. New York: Semiotext(e).

Virilio, P. 1995. *Open Sky*. London: Verso.

Whannel, G. 1992. *Fields in Vision: Television Sport and Cultural Transformation*. London: Routledge.

Weinrich, H. 1970. 'Tense and Time'. *Archivum Linguisticum* 1, pp. 31–42.

Willett, T. 1988. 'A Cross-Linguistic Survey of the Grammaticalization of Evidentiality'. *Studies in Language* 12, pp. 51–97.

Winston, B. 2002. 'Towards Tabloidization? Glasgow Revisited, 1975–2001'. *Journalism Studies* 3(1), pp. 5–20.

Zettl, H. 1978. 'The Rare Case of Television Aesthetics'. *Journal of the University Film Association* 30(2), pp. 3–8.

Index